Digital Tools for
Knowledge Construction
in the Elementary Grades

Digital Tools for Knowledge Construction in the Elementary Grades

Michael Blocher

ROWMAN & LITTLEFIELD
Lanham • Boulder • New York • London

Published by Rowman & Littlefield
A wholly owned subsidiary of The Rowman & Littlefield Publishing Group, Inc.
4501 Forbes Boulevard, Suite 200, Lanham, Maryland 20706
www.rowman.com

Unit A, Whitacre Mews, 26-34 Stannary Street, London SE11 4AB

British Library Cataloguing in Publication Information Available

Library of Congress Cataloging-in-Publication Data Available
ISBN: 978-1-4758-2849-8 (cloth : alk. paper)
ISBN: 978-1-4758-2850-4 (pbk. : alk. paper)
ISBN: 978-1-4758-2851-1 (electronic)

∞ ™ The paper used in this publication meets the minimum requirements of American
National Standard for Information Sciences—Permanence of Paper for Printed Library
Materials, ANSI/NISO Z39.48-1992.

Printed in the United States of America

Contents

Preface

Often, when people think about integrating technology into learning, they think about how technology might be *used* within the classroom. One such way is when the teacher uses technology for classroom management, such as by entering student information, grades, and attendance into the school's networked computer. Other ways include projecting a presentation of content through SMART Boards®; having students work at the computer to complete self-paced instructional programs; or using iPads, tablets, or smartphones to practice skills such as math.

The purpose of this book is to provide teachers with some ideas on how to integrate technology into their classroom instruction in ways that support student-centered learning. This does not mean having the teacher use presentation tools to impart information to students. Rather, it involves a more student-centered approach that engages students in activities where they can use digital tools to construct meaningful products, thereby enabling them to further enhance their existing knowledge.

An easy way to think about this is to visualize which way the information or knowledge is flowing. If a teacher is using SMART Boards® to teach, although it may help students pay attention, the information is still flowing from teacher to student, thereby putting the teacher at the center and in charge of the learning activity. To be sure, there are appropriate times for this manner of teaching. But if the student is using the SMART Board®, then he or she takes center stage and controls the learning activity.

Think about it one step further. When students use digital tools to create meaningful artifacts that focus on academic content, they organize their background knowledge and assimilate or accommodate any new information into

the construction of that artifact, be it a presentation, movie, or any other published product. Student-created digital products can be assessed for achievement when the criteria are properly aligned to academic standards. The focus
of this book is to do just that: to engage students using digital tools so that it
puts them at the center of the learning process and gives them more control.

Introduction

This text is divided into two parts. Part I provides a foundation for technology integration into classroom instruction, including (a) a perspective and rationale of student-centered learning, (b) instructional strategies for technology integration, and (c) academic standards and assessment as they relate to relates to technology integration within student-centered learning approaches. Part II is structured so that each chapter focuses on a specific topic that provides teachers with information, methods, and examples of integrating technology in a student-centered approach.

Part II begins with information on basic technology operations and global digital citizenship. These topics provide a foundation for the remaining chapters that discuss how students can appropriately use digital tools for learning through communication and collaboration, research, data collection and analysis, publishing, critical thinking, problem-solving, and gaming. Each chapter in Part II provides a contextually based elementary classroom scenario that illustrates the chapter's topic. These scenarios provide examples of the learners using digital tools that help them meet national standards and achieve elementary-grade-level objectives/outcomes.

The rapid advancements in technology make writing a book of this nature challenging because current tools may be replaced with newer versions or totally new applications. To help overcome this challenge, this book often refers to software and hardware simply as digital tools. However, there are also many examples of specific digital tools that are used to provide context. Therefore, as teachers read through this book, it's important for them to think about each tool's concept or function, rather than the specific tool described. If a scenario suggests that students use MS Word, don't think that it has to be that actual product. Think about it as a word processor, or, better yet, as a publishing tool. Another example is if a scenario identifies a specific cognitive mapping software (i.e., Inspiration), think about any digital device that can help visualize ideas and organize thoughts.

Thinking in terms of the concept being discussed rather than a specific digital tool or software will also help teachers keep pace with changes in technology. In other words, rather than focusing on the tool itself, they should focus on the purpose of the examples in this book and how they demonstrate technology integration in ways that support student-centered learning.

Part I

FOUNDATIONS

Part I provides an introduction, rationale, and perspective of student-centered technology integration, instructional strategies, and assessment as it relates to elementary learners.

Chapter 1

Perspective

Today's teachers are expected to understand how to utilize technology to enhance the learning environment within their classrooms. Technology integration can be defined as a way to support and enhance classroom management, instructional delivery, and student engagement.

This chapter will introduce you to technology integration from two opposing perspectives of learning: objectivism and constructivism. Comparing and contrasting these two perspectives will, hopefully, provide an illustration of how a teacher's perspective of learning might impact his or her instructional decisions while integrating technology. As teachers read through this chapter, they need to try and reflect on what they think about learning, how best they learn, and how they think their students can best learn. They also need to think about how the methods they employ might impact what technology tools they might use and how they will be used within the classroom.

PERSPECTIVE OF LEARNING

Educational researchers and writers often disagree on learning theories that describe how students learn best. Because we all have had different learning experiences and learn in different ways, one teacher's perspective of learning often differs greatly from another's. A teacher's perspective and, consequently, how he or she approaches classroom tasks, is based upon his or her understanding of learning theories as well as personal learning experiences.

Even though many might agree that integrating technology into the classroom can enhance the learning environment, many teachers may have different ideas about how to do so. Most would agree that teachers need to have a rationale for why and how to integrate technology. They need to plan how

3

to best engage their students with technology tools, rather than simply using technology for technology's sake.

It is important to understand one's perspective of learning because it will impact *how* and *why* one integrates technology. To gain a better understanding of how a teacher's perspective of learning might impact how he or she approaches the classroom, here's an example of opposing perspectives as described by early leaders in the field of educational technology.

Vrasidas (2000) compared two contrasting points of view that we can use to help understand different ways to integrate technology. Figure 1.1 illustrates two opposing perspectives of learning in an objectivism–constructivism continuum.

Figure 1.2 includes elements that might help you think about how these opposing perspectives could impact one's approach to learning. For example, objectivists are more inclined to take what can be defined as a "teacher-centered" approach to learning where the teacher has more responsibility and controls the classroom. On the contrary, constructivists are more likely to take what can be defined as the "student-centered" approach, where the student has more responsibility and control over his or her learning.

While there are opposite ends displayed on the continuum, most teachers would describe themselves as somewhere between objectivism and constructivism, rather than being at one end or the other. For example, there may be times when a teacher might use an instructional strategy that could be perceived as coming from an objectivist's perspective, even though he or she might consider himself or herself a constructivist. A teacher's approach to learning may not be as black and white as one might think. To help frame technology integration, let's compare and contrast these two opposing perspectives from each end.

For the sake of gaining a better understanding of integrating technology, think of them in stark contrast. While this is overly simplified, it may help if teachers think about their perspective of learning by comparing and contrasting two very different points of view. Analyzing these two perspectives in

Figure 1.1   Perspective Continuum

Objectivism		Constructivism
Teacher Centered		Student Centered
Teacher Control		Student Control
Teacher Responsibility		Student Responsibility

Figure 1.2   Teacher-Centered vs. Student-Centered

this simplistic manner will provide discussion points to help them think about technology integration.

Objectivism

From this perspective, one might believe that knowledge is being cognizant of facts, skills, and concepts as they relate to what is true, making knowledge bound and confined to specifics. Perhaps the main belief here is that knowledge is thought to be a deliverable, which can be transmitted from teacher to student. For example, students gain knowledge of grammar when a teacher provides his or her students with a list of rules for grammar. Similarly, students learn fractions after practicing the steps that have been instructed to them. Often referred to as an objectivist perspective, this suggests that knowledge is something that is transferable between the knowledge-giver and knowledge-recipient.

Constructivism

In contrast, constructivists believe that knowledge is constructed by the student, not received from a teacher, instructor, or computer program. Learning is a much more complex process than just receiving a set of facts, concepts, or definitions that are simply to be stored in memory. Learning is the construction of knowledge, or the understanding and skills that students build while engaged in experiences where they are thinking about or exploring ideas as they relate to their current surroundings.

This viewpoint of learning and knowledge construction is often referred to as the constructivist perspective and suggests that human learning is the process of building new knowledge upon the foundation of previous knowledge. From this perspective, the student is responsible for constructing the knowledge. The teacher or instructor is responsible for providing an engaging learning environment that includes support and scaffolds when needed.

Constructionism

When we think about constructivism, especially when we think of utilizing technology tools to promote student engagement, educational technologists often also use the term constructionism. Papert (1993) suggests that constructionism supports constructivism but that learning is enhanced when learners are engaged in the *process of construction*. As Papert (1991) stated:

> Constructionism . . . shares constructivism's connotation of learning as "building knowledge structures" irrespective of the circumstances of the learning.

It then adds the idea that this happens especially felicitously in a context where the learner is consciously engaged in constructing a public entity, whether it's a sand castle on the beach or a theory of the universe. (p. 1)

Distributed Constructionism

Resnick (1996) defined distributed constructionism as a process wherein learners utilize computer networking technology to support distributed construction through discussions, sharing, and collaborations. In other words, they benefit from the use of technology that supports collaborative "design and construction activities" (p. 281) to actively engage in the construction of personally meaningful products.

This requires the cognitive engagement of the student, which is more complex than the mere building of new knowledge by engaging in the construction of things. Specifically, Resnick (1996) stated, "What's important is that they are actively engaged in creating something that is meaningful to themselves or to others around them" (p. 281).

The importance of meaningful learning is echoed by Jonassen, Peck, and Wilson (1999) who provide specific elements of meaningful learning. They suggest that meaningful learning is fostered when students are:

- Actively interacting and being able to observe their manipulating elements within the learning environment;
- Constructing individual mental models based upon their experiences and interpretations with prior knowledge;
- Intentionally setting goals, selecting strategies, and making decisions about learning;
- Authentically situated in some meaningful, real-world task or setting; and
- Cooperating, collaborating, and socially negotiating within groups working on common tasks.

Integrating specific technology tools into the learning environment can support these elements in various ways. For example, interactive visualization software such as Geometer's Sketchpad® provides opportunities for students to manipulate geometric shapes and then observe changes of angles and lengths based upon their manipulations. Cognitive mapping tools, such as Inspiration®, encourage students to construct mental models of ideas and concepts or to list and organize background knowledge and learning experiences to help them set goals, select strategies, and make decisions.

Internet resources and communication tools can be used to gather data and communicate with experts on real-world topics and issues. Social media and collaborative electronic tools promote cooperation, collaboration, and social negotiations within groups of students as they coauthor papers and reports.

Think about how the technology tools described above can support learning as it might relate to how one's perspective of learning can impact how technology might be integrated within the classroom environment.

INTEGRATING TECHNOLOGY

There are several ways that teachers can integrate technology within their classroom. For example, students can learn *about* technology, they can learn *from* technology, and they can learn *with* technology (Jonassen et al., 2003).

First, students can learn *about* technology by developing an understanding that helps them use the computer. For example, they learn how to use the current operating system to navigate the computer, run various applications, create and save files, and possibly even to communicate with others. Understanding the computer and its workings constitute knowledge and skills that are often defined as computer literacy.

Because technology changes very quickly, learning about technology is an ongoing process. Even the most highly computer-literate people may need to brush up their knowledge of technology at various times. Over the years, there have been many substantial changes with new versions of operating systems and productivity tools. Even technology veterans can be left scratching their heads at times. Good problem-solving skills coupled with trial-and-error methods can be invaluable when learning *about* technology.

Second, students can learn *from* technology when it is used to deliver or present specific instruction or content through a computer, tablet, or even a smartphone. An example of such learning is when a teacher uses a presentation tool to create a slide show as a visual aid to support a direct instructional lesson.

A better example might be when students interact with a computer program, such as in a computer-based instructional (CBI) module. Here, students are given instructions through computers programmed with content or activities to help them gain specific knowledge or be able to perform certain skills. These are often self-paced and controlled by the learner's ability to answer content questions.

Finally, students can learn *with* technology when technology tools are utilized to support and enhance the learning environment. There are many ways that a teacher can engage his or her students with technology tools. The key, however, is that when students learn *with* technology they are generally using tools to support their investigation, visualization, or creations that help demonstrate their acquired knowledge.

This is by far the most complex of the three purposes of classroom technology integration, as there are many different types of technology tools that can be used in very different ways, now available to the teacher. As you read the next section, try to think about how these two perspectives are fundamentally quite different.

Technology Integration from the Objectivist's Perspective

Technology integration from an objectivist's perspective will most probably include the use of tools that maintain the viewpoint that knowledge is transferable, which would, therefore, include tools and software applications, like CBI programs discussed above, that deliver content to the students.

In some cases, students interact with the computer program in a very structured and linear manner, in a way that directs them through each screen in a very specific order, leaving them little or no control over their learning. Other programs are less linear and provide some degree of student control perhaps through menus of choice by which they select the information, content, or scenarios they wish to access.

As students select specific topics and go through the material, there can be additional screens that ask them to interact in some way to demonstrate that they have learned that content. These interactions could be in the form of multiple choice questions, fill in the blanks, or click an object and drag it to the appropriate location. More recent and sophisticated programs can even provide for an "intelligent element" that first identifies the level of skill or knowledge based upon the students' input and then chooses and delivers the appropriate (more difficult or less difficult) level of instruction or interactive activities.

In this way, such programs guide students through the learning process at their individual learning pace or level. For example, with more input from a student (i.e., clicking on a choice, providing a correct or incorrect answer to a question), the computer program provides remediation, further instruction, or possibly feedback on his or her progress. Even though these programs might provide for greater student control, the instruction is still delivered to the student, and as such, suggests that integrating technology in this manner is from an objectivist perspective.

However, it can be less explicit than that. For example, one might use the Internet, a vast storehouse of content information, to simply deliver information to the student. In this example, the content to be learned would be delivered by simply reading the information provided by the web pages. Although the student has some control over the flow of information, or even perhaps, the type of media that is used to deliver the information, similar to learning from technology described above, the general flow of information is from the technology tool to the student.

Another example might include multimedia encyclopedias that provide audio and video delivery of content to the student. Software of this nature might even provide interaction where students are required to engage with the media, clicking on elements within the program that would bring up information or content in various media formats, based upon their individual preferences. Even though students may have some control over the type and perhaps even the content delivered, they are still recipients, receiving pages of text, narration, or video that provides them with information.

While this is a very limited description of the objectivist's perspective of technology integration, it provides a contrasting point upon which to discuss the constructivist's perspective. As you read through the next section try to remember how the objectivist perspective views knowledge as facts, skills, and concepts and learning as the acquiring or receiving of that knowledge from someone or something outside of him or herself. Learning, even with some student control, is still delivered to the student, rather than being generated by the student.

Technology Integration from the Constructivist's Perspective

Technology integration from a constructivist's perspective would most likely require students to be active participants in their use of technology tools to explore concepts, gather data, test hypotheses, and publish and share findings, thereby, constructing their understanding.

From a distributed constructionist's approach, one might engage students to work together as members of a team to investigate and solve authentic, real-world problems, like global warming, by utilizing various technology tools such as visualization, exploration, publishing, communication, and perhaps simulations to engage in knowledge construction, in a process that can be defined as meaningful learning.

In this example, while students might utilize Internet resources, it would be for more than simply retrieving information. Here, they would be asked to judge the retrieved information for accuracy and/or reliability. They would then analyze findings and apply the newly acquired information to help support their conjectures and ideas. They might communicate with experts in the field to gain information and perhaps differing perspectives on the topic. They might also employ multimedia authoring tools to generate, publish, and share meaningful products as an alternative assessment of their learning.

By integrating technology into learning environments from this perspective, students have the opportunity to work together to assemble and share their understandings of new concepts and ideas as they build upon their previous knowledge. Thus, they are learning *with* technology from a constructivist perspective. To integrate technology in this way, teachers must be able to select technology tools and plan instructional strategies that utilize these tools in an intentional manner to help their students achieve the objectives or outcomes designed for a lesson.

There are a variety of technology tools that support various instructional strategies and a variety of learning activities such as practicing, creating, organizing, researching, communicating, exploring, thinking, planning, and visualizing. Integrating technology means that the teacher must select and plan the use of a specific tool that will best support the learning task. It also means that the teacher must decide on an instructional strategy where students use that tool within the classroom environment in ways that enhance learning and best support achievement of the objectives, outcomes, or goals for that lesson.

As one might imagine, this is a complex task that requires sophisticated knowledge of the software and their implementation in learning environments. Maddux, Johnson, and Willis (2001) defined software used in education as Type I or Type II applications. These definitions help teachers understand how software applications differ and help them select one over another.

Type I Applications

These applications are generally educational software programs designed to provide information to the student. If there are opportunities for student input, they are generally more directed, highly structured, and less open-ended. The software requires specific but limited student input. This can be the case even in a simulation tool where the software developer predetermines almost everything that happens on the screen. Generally, this type of application is aimed at the introduction to or the acquisition of facts by rote memory through drill and practice.

A teacher might integrate this type of application to introduce specific concepts to students, which may be fairly concrete or limited, or have them practice previously introduced skills. As you think about Type I applications, think about the direction of information. In a Type I application, information generally flows toward, or is delivered to, the student.

Type II Applications

Type II applications generally are more open-ended and require much more active intellectual involvement, in terms of higher-level thinking, on the part of the student. These applications may be productivity tools that students use to create or construct a product that provides them the opportunity to demonstrate their understanding of skills or concepts. Students have more control over the interactions between themselves and the computer, which often requires greater engagement from them.

These applications are usually aimed at accomplishing more creative tasks than Type I. For example, a teacher might integrate Type II applications to support students in their investigation of information, analyses of data, drawing of conclusions, solving of problems, and presenting/publishing their findings.

As you think about Type II applications, rather than thinking about the direction of information as you did with Type I applications, think about students using the technology as an intelligent tool to help them build or enhance their knowledge about any particular content or topic. In this way, the technology tool could be seen as a collaborator helping and supporting students in the task of learning.

Mindtools

Jonassen uses the term "Mindtools" to suggest that technology tools can be used for constructive learning, stating, "Mindtools are computer-based tools and learning environments that have been adapted or developed to function as intellectual partners with the learner in order to engage and facilitate critical thinking and higher order learning" (2000, p. 9). Technology integration from this perspective engages students in the creative process by making them utilize tools to help them construct knowledge.

Mindtools should be utilized to engage the learner in critical thinking, where they do more than just produce. They should be utilized for organizing, modeling, visualizing, constructing, and conversing. For example, word processors are *not* Mindtools, as Jonassen defines them because "they do not significantly restructure and amplify the thinking of the learner or the capabilities afforded by that thinking. Word processing does not restructure the task of writing" (2000, p. 16). Although word processors provide an easy-to-use tool to help one get their ideas onto paper, they don't enhance the student's thinking about what he or she is writing, nor his or her ability to write well.

Other applications within productivity suites (i.e., MS Office, Open Office), including database and spreadsheet programs, according to Jonassen, "can also function as cognitive tools for enhancing, extending, amplifying, and restructuring the way learners think about the content they are studying. These applications provide alternative conceptualizations of the content for the learner. They provide new formalisms for thinking. That makes them Mindtools" (2000, p. 16).

Integrating software like MicroWorlds (i.e., Logo®) could be considered a Mindtool, because it can provide students with the opportunity to explore, interact, and build scenarios wherein they can manipulate variables and observe outcomes. By interacting in this way, students can "visually" construct their own mental models of complex real-world concepts, thus learning new ways of thinking about them. Communication and publishing software could also be considered Mindtools because they encourage students working together to assemble artifacts that support their understanding of concepts as they construct elements, adding detail to their mental models.

SUMMARY

The purpose of this chapter was to help teachers gain a better understanding of technology integration and perhaps its complexity. Teachers are expected to be technologically savvy and proficient at integrating technology to support their classrooms in three ways: (a) classroom management, (b) instructional delivery, and (c) student engagement. As such, teachers should be proficient in utilizing several technology tools to enhance their classrooms in a variety of ways, which requires them to continue learning how to use the ever-growing list of new technologies.

Objectivism and constructivism were presented in very contrasting ways to provide explicit and distinct examples to help them better understand how technology can be integrated from a teacher-directed to a student-centered perspective. Although it is an oversimplified way to think about this, the objectivist–constructivist continuum presented might be helpful in thinking about the different ways by which technology can be integrated.

Classroom teachers should have a rationale for why and how they are integrating technology to best engage their students with the technology tools— depending upon the instructional purpose. Technology integration decisions, like all instructional decisions, should be done thoughtfully. When teachers integrate technology to present information, knowledge is being transmitted from the teacher to the learner. Technology is being integrated in a more teacher-directed manner, where the teacher is in control of the information dissemination. There are times when using technology to support direct instruction is desired and appropriate.

There will also be times when learners can use technology tools to explore new ideas, analyze data, investigate problems, organize information, and/

or present findings, which engages them in an active way, thus encouraging them to acquire, assimilate, and build or enhance understandings and skills. In this manner, the *learners* are more in control and taking responsibility for their learning. Integrating technology through Type II applications from a constructivist's perspective requires that teachers relinquish the more traditional role of being the giver of knowledge and help the student take on the responsibility for their learning.

This chapter compared and contrasted technology integration in terms of the objectivist–constructivist continuum. By offering an overview of these two competing approaches to learning, and by asking teachers to reflect on their own philosophy of learning, it is my hope that they gained a broader understanding of the variety of ways they might integrate technology. It is hoped that they also gained an understanding of the importance of knowing how and why they might use technology tools within the classroom.

REFERENCES

Jonassen, D. H. (2000). *Computers as mindtools for schools: Engaging critical thinking*, second ed. Upper Saddle River, NJ: Prentice Hall.

Jonassen, D. H., Peck, K. C., and Wilson, B. G. (1999). *Learning with technology: A constructivist perspective*. Upper Saddle River, NJ: Prentice Hall.

Jonassen, D., Howland, J., Moore, J., and Marra, R. (2003). *Learning to solve problems with technology*. Upper Saddle River, NJ: Prentice Hall.

Maddux, C. C., Johnson, D. L., and Willis, J. W. (2001). *Educational computing: Learning with tomorrow's technologies* (third ed.). Needham Heights, MA: Allyn & Bacon.

Papert, S. (1991). Situating Constructionism. In I. A. Harel, *Constructionism* (p. 1). Norwood, NJ: Ablex.

Papert, S. (1993). *The children's machine: Rethinking school in the age of the computer*. New York, NY: Basic Books.

Resnick, M. (1996). *Distributed Constructionism*. Proceedings of the International Conference of the Learning Sciences, Northwestern University.

Vrasidas, C. (2000). Constructivism versus objectivism: Implications for interaction, course design, and evaluation in distance education. *International Journal of Educational Telecommunications*, 6 (4), 339–62.

Chapter 2

Instructional Strategies

Teachers feel and are held responsible for their students' learning. Yet, if they believe that students construct knowledge, they must also then provide the freedom for their students to manage and take responsibility for that learning. As one might imagine, each teacher must come to some level of comfort in the balancing act of designing and managing learning activities that provide enough structure to support the students, while at the same time providing opportunities for their students to construct knowledge.

This may cause teachers to find themselves at a very interesting *point of tension* between being responsible for their students' learning and at the same time being able to give them freedom and opportunity to take control of their learning. Since the teacher designs instructions and/or plans lessons, aren't they in control of the learning? If so, how can they provide a student-centered learning environment? Fortunately, there are instructional strategies that classroom teachers use in conjunction with the use of technology tools that help them in that balancing act.

The purpose of this chapter is to describe several instructional strategies as they relate to technology integration. In doing so, it is hoped that teachers will gain a better understanding of various strategies that will support their instructional decisions as they begin to think about organizing and managing their classrooms and how they will integrate technology into their teaching practice.

INSTRUCTIONAL STRATEGIES

Take a moment to think about the different types of learning experiences that you've had to this point in your life, think about the instructional strategies or approaches to which you've been exposed. For example, as a university student you may have called your university faculty "instructors." To help you achieve greater success in learning one of your more difficult subjects you might have hired a "tutor." Or, to better perform some specific task or sport you may have worked with a "trainer."

While we may use different terms for each of these types of educators, they all have one goal in common: to improve a student's understanding, knowledge, or skill. However, each of these terms may have a specific connotation, which is often based upon how these educators approach their task. In thinking about each of these approaches, try to remember how each might be similar or different to that of the "teachers" you had while attending pre-K–12 school.

Instructor

The term "instructor" is used to describe one who "instructs" or imparts knowledge in a systematic way. Indeed, when we think of "reading the instructions" we often think of reading a list of steps to be performed to learn how to operate something. An instructor can provide instruction to individual students, but more often delivers lectures and assigns class homework, which requires textbook readings or researching other resources, to a larger group to help them learn course concepts and content. While a classroom teacher may often provide instruction, they are generally not called instructors.

Tutor

The term "tutor" is used to describe one who provides more individual help for students who may have specific needs or difficulties learning specific concepts or content. Many college students have helped defray some of their college expenses by "tutoring" some of their peers struggling to prepare for an upcoming test or lab exercise.

By gaining individual help, the student is more able to ask questions and get answers to help them gain a better understanding of difficult material. While we don't necessarily think of classroom teachers as tutors, they often act in that manner. Think about how a teacher can provide individual help that is needed at just the right moment.

Trainer and Coach

The term "training" is used to describe how one gains skills by instruction, discipline, exercise, and/or drill. For example, the term "trainer" is often used to describe one who helps prepare athletes to perform at a higher level, through drill and practice. Similarly, the term "coach" is used to describe those who help athletes improve their skills by supporting them with direction, feedback, and encouragement. Indeed, gymnastic coaches often provide physical support by holding an arm or leg of their athletes as they begin learning to use the balance beam.

Teacher

The term "teacher" is generally used to describe educators who work with pre-K–12 students. However, there are times that a classroom teacher may perform many of the roles just described. Teachers act as instructors who design and deliver instruction. They act as trainers who provide exercises and drills to help improve their students' skills. They also coach their students with supportive encouragement and appropriate comments. Finally, they act as tutors who provide individual help. In this way, teachers often use various educational approaches that help their students learn in a variety of ways.

BALANCING ACT AT THE POINT OF TENSION

Let's look at the example of a child learning to ride a bicycle to illustrate how a teacher might act in all of these roles. When a child is learning to move beyond a tricycle to ride a "two-wheeler," training wheels are often used. They are designed to provide stability for the child as he or she begins learning to ride a bicycle. However, they are also designed to be adjustable to allow for various levels of support.

As the child begins to ride the bicycle, the training wheels can be set at the same level as the main rear wheel. This supports the child in a way so that he or she will not lean nor fall to one side or the other when standing still or just starting out. As the child begins to feel more comfortable and is able to go faster, the training wheels can be raised a bit at a time. This allows the child to begin to take control of the bike, in terms of turning by leaning left or right, but still being balanced. Eventually, the child becomes comfortable balancing the bike to the point that the training wheels are removed as they are no longer necessary.

While this is a good way to help support the child when he or she is learning, it is important for the parent to observe and make sure that they are adjusting the training wheels up at the right time. Each child learns to do this at different ages, some more quickly and some more slowly. If, for example, the parent raises the training wheels too soon, the child may lose confidence in his or her ability to balance the bike.

However, unless the training wheels are raised the child will simply ride the bicycle in the same manner that he or she rode a tricycle. The child will not learn to lean the bike to turn, but will rather simply turn the handle bars and thus not gain an understanding of the dynamics and balance of riding a bicycle.

In this example, the parent would probably begin teaching his or her child to ride first by giving some *instructions* on the purpose of the training wheels; how they would help in stability, how the child might begin to ride using them, and how the wheels would be raised as progress was made in learning to ride. Next, the parent would act as a *coach* by providing support while the child climbs onto the bike. The parent would then encourage the child to help boost confidence.

As the parent observes the child's progress he or she might ask if it is time to raise the training wheels. Because every child learns at his or her own pace, each is individually *tutored* by the parent. The child negotiates the raising of the training wheels to the point when they are no longer necessary and he or she has learned to successfully ride the bike.

Similarly, teachers use various educational approaches as described here. For example, they often begin by giving their students instructions or directions. They then provide support, scaffolds, resources, and materials. Because some learners learn more quickly than others, the teacher must observe and be aware of their students' individual needs. Then, like the parent with the decision of raising or removing the training wheels, teachers must also make decisions that best suits each student's learning.

Teachers want to provide students with the necessary support for their learning, but at the same time give them the freedom to take control and responsibility of their own learning. Some students will need additional scaffolds (i.e., individual *tutoring*, additional practice and/or resources, *coaching*, and *encouragement*). It is this decision point that creates the *point of tension* for teachers.

TECHNOLOGY INTEGRATION IN A STUDENT-CENTERED APPROACH

Teachers who adopt a more student-centered approach often integrate technology in situations where students actively use digital tools to help them construct knowledge. There are several ways in which technology can be integrated that support a student-centered approach. In this section we'll discuss, how to engage students in safe but real-life settings where they work together to produce products, complete tasks, and solve problems as they build and demonstrate their understanding of learning standards as they can be developed, embedded within the context of real-life situations and simulations.

In a student-centered approach, technology tools can be used to help students examine a case, make inquiry into topics, collect and analyze data, visualize solutions to a problem, and construct products that demonstrate their understandings. In other words, technology tools are used to engage and support students in their research, in the analysis of their findings, and in the application of their knowledge and skills to some outcome rather than simply being used to present them with information and concepts.

Student-centered approaches can still vary in how much structure the teacher provides and how much responsibility he or she requires of his or her students. The role of the teacher may still vary greatly in terms of the support, resources, and help or scaffolds that are provided to help students be successful in their learning environment. While reading through this section, pay particular attention to how you might feel in terms of the *point of tension* as it relates to the methods and strategies described.

Case-Based, Project-Based, and Inquiry-Based Learning

Case-based learning, project-based learning, and inquiry-based learning are clearly defined instructional strategies that are considered to be student-centered. Rather than simply presenting or delivering information and concepts, in these learning approaches, students are engaged in research of some kind, analyzing findings, and applying their knowledge and skills to visualize solutions. In doing so, students use technology tools in a similar way to those who solve real-world problems by identifying task assignments, organizing work flow, and communicating with peers.

In these approaches the teacher must still provide information, guidance, and structure, by playing the role of a facilitator who encourages and expects students to engage in critical and higher-order thinking. The level of structure and guidance often is dependent on the instructional approaches of the teacher in terms of the point of tension.

Case-based learning provides a "case" within a context that includes real-life situations. Students are given the opportunity to develop and practice their ability to think critically and apply the required knowledge and skills to work the case. If the case results in a group or team project, the teacher may provide guidance in teaming strategies or help students develop their roles within their groups to facilitate better communication and task completion.

Project-based learning is similar in that students are engaged in activities that require collaboration, although the activity is more structured and students generally follow procedures or steps to help them work collaboratively to construct a product. In this approach, however, when students encounter problems, the teacher's role is "more likely to be instructor and coach (rather than tutors) who provide expert guidance, feedback and suggestions for 'better' ways to achieve the final product" (Savery, 2006, p. 16).

Inquiry-based learning is probably the most similar to problem-based learning (PBL) in that students are given a question upon which they gather information and think critically to investigate solutions. Again, the role of the teacher is less like the role of tutor in a PBL approach. Here the teacher can provide direction and information that will help them answer the question at hand. Even though this approach provides more structure or control, the teacher will still need to make instructional decisions that are likely to cause tension.

Problem-Based Learning

Problem-based learning is similar to case-based, project-based, and inquiry-based learning. Here, students are given an *ill-structured problem* and work in teams to try and find a solution or set of solutions that are based on their research, understanding of theory, and application of knowledge and skills. However there are fundamental differences, primarily in how much structure is provided and the role of the teacher. "While cases and projects are excellent learner-centered instructional strategies, they tend to diminish the learner's role in setting the goals and outcomes for the 'problem.'" (Savery, 2006, p. 16). Characteristics of PBL clearly identify "(1) the role of the tutor as a facilitator of learning, (2) the responsibilities of the learners to be self-directed and selfregulated in their learning, and (3) the essential elements in the design of ill-structured instructional problems as the driving force for inquiry" (p. 15).

The selection of the ill-structured problem is a key element, as it is the foundation of the PBL approach. The problem presented to the students should be real-world in that there should be no defined solutions, thus requiring greater inquiry and engagement into the topic to develop a solution. If the problem is too structured, the students may be less apt to engage fully. Because the PBL approach focuses on the student being responsible and self-directing his or her learning, the role of the teacher becomes critical as well. In a PBL approach, the teacher guides the learning process and provides a debriefing from the role of *tutor*.

Being an effective tutor when using a PBL approach places the responsibility of learning on the students. In addition to gathering information and answers to help solve the problem, students are also given responsibility for group organization, role and task assignments, and to plan all of the elements, including selecting the technology tools for research, analysis, and presentation. As a PBL *tutor*, the teacher is less directive and simply provides a mirror for students to help them understand their thinking processes, thereby also helping them reflect on the problem-solving process.

As one might imagine, this approach requires considerable support materials and scaffolds to be available to the students in several skill areas. In all probability, it will include scaffolds for teaming, self-directed or self-regulated learning, and of course problem-solving (Savery, 2006). As technology is integrated into the PBL approach, students will probably also need scaffolds in (a) information on what technology tools might be best to use for a specific task, and (b) skills on using the tools.

Making the transition from being the knowledge-giver to being a tutor who helps facilitate learning in a PBL approach is challenging (Ertmer and Simons, 2006), and deciding and providing the appropriate scaffolds when implementing this approach is likely to cause the point of tension for the classroom teacher.

Collaborative and Cooperative Learning

A student-centered approach often utilizes collaborative learning and/or cooperative learning methods. There are varying descriptions and details of how collaborative and cooperative learning differ. For example, Roschelle and Teasley (1995) state that collaboration suggests that students coordinate to accomplish a task.

Cooperation, on the other hand, requires that tasks are partitioned and each individual is responsible for some aspect that adds to the whole project or task. Panitz (1996) suggests that cooperation is when students work together within a structured learning environment that supports the completion of an end product or task. Collaboration, on the other hand, is viewed as a personal lifestyle or philosophy. Slavin (1997) views cooperative learning as it relates to ill-structured domains and collaboration as it relates better to well-structured domains.

However, there are common elements that exist between the two and they can be identified as follows:

- Learning takes place in an active mode;
- The teacher is more a facilitator than a "sage on the stage";
- Teaching and learning are shared experiences between teachers and students;
- Students participate in small-group activities;
- Students must take responsibility for learning;
- Discussing and articulating one's ideas in a small-group setting enhances the student's ability to reflect on his or her own assumptions and thought processes;
- Students develop social and team skills through the give-and-take of consensus-building;

- Students profit from belonging to a small and supportive academic community; and
- Students experience diversity which is essential in a multicultural democracy (Matthews et al., 1995, pp. 34–40).

With that in mind, however, let's take a look at some of the important elements that are essential for designing cooperative learning activities. Roseth, Garfield, and Ben-Zvi (2008) argue that the most important aspect of implementing a cooperative learning activity is in providing the instructions of how and what students have to do. Specifically, they suggest that the instructor: (a) group the students, (b) provide specific criteria to successfully complete the activity, and (c) provide a structure that connects individual students to the activity goals.

The group size of students can be a crucial element. Groups could range from two to six, but generally work best if they are smaller than larger. Remember the old adage "Too many cooks spoil the broth?" However, groups should be large enough to complete the activity. Think about the tasks that you need to have completed through cooperative learning and how long it might take to complete. Think about how many students might be the best number to work together on it.

You probably have been grouped in cooperative learning activities where you ended up doing the lion's share of the work, or, perhaps, you may have felt guilty for not doing your fair share of the work. This happens more often than not. While some students may have the ability to manage groups by creating their own roles and identifying responsibilities to distribute the workload, many do not. Linking individual students to specific products or tasks can be vital if the teacher wants to ensure an equitable workload in completing the cooperative learning activity.

By designing *individual accountability* into cooperative learning activities, the teacher makes each member of the team responsible for some element of the final product or artifact. This provides the structure that helps the students know what needs to be done and who will do what. For example, teachers might design specific roles or jobs that are responsible for specific tasks that will help add to the final completed project.

While making students in a cooperative learning group individually accountable, it is also very important to ensure that they cooperative with one another. The point of a cooperative learning activity is for students to work together. In other words, they need to depend upon each other in their team. By including *positive group interdependence* into cooperative learning activities, teachers insist that the team works together to complete the learning task.

Teachers may want to provide the structure that will help the students work together successfully by making it clear that each person in the team is not only responsible for learning the material in the learning activity *but* also for helping their teammates learn as well. By designing an activity where each student's task is part of the final completed project, students must work together to assemble the completed project from the individual parts. In addition, providing some element of motivation for the success of the entire team helps students realize their responsibilities toward cooperating with and helping their fellow students.

PROVIDING HELP AND SUPPORT: SCAFFOLDS

When students work together, many often need help in a variety of ways, such as in organizing their teams, getting ideas on the best way to approach their line of inquiry, analyzing and sharing their findings, not to mention understanding concepts or using a technology tool. This is generally called providing scaffolds. The term "scaffold" was first coined by Wood et al. (1974). It has been used to describe assistance or tutoring to help support students gain an understanding that they might not otherwise attain.

Similar to the training wheel example used earlier in this chapter, scaffolds are provided by a teacher or peer while students are just learning concepts and tasks. Once the student has an understanding of the material, scaffolds are no longer needed and are taken away. They are often necessary in student-centered activities when students need support in a variety of ways. In particular, when integrating technology, students might need to have what Saye and Brush (2002) describe as "hard scaffolds" that "are static supports that can be anticipated and planned in advance based on typical student difficulties with a task" (p. 81).

Educational software may have hard scaffolds built into the application, in terms of particular tools that students might use to gain support when having anticipated difficulties or additional needs. For example, a multimedia learning program may include links to tools that help students organize and prioritize information. This type of scaffold helps them structure the information so they can gain a better understanding of the material. However, one could also argue that a hard scaffold could also be templates for student-produced products that help provide structure and guide students in completing a required task.

In addition to hard scaffolds, Saye and Brush (2002) also state that "soft scaffolds are dynamic and situational. Soft scaffolding requires teachers to continuously diagnose the understandings of learners and provide timely support based on student responses" (p. 82). Because this type of scaffolding is specific to the context and situation, it could be more difficult to provide, but, if given in a timely fashion, will support the students at their time of need. However, this type of scaffolding is dependent upon teachers who can identify and analyze a student's or a team's needs based on their questions, responses, or perhaps just keen observations.

Soft scaffolding could require the teacher to act as an instructor, tutor, or coach. In doing so, the teacher may need to provide instruction, advice, facilitate ideas, and/or direct the student or a group of students to resources or hard scaffolds that will help them be more successful in completing the task, solving the problem, working in cooperation, and/or demonstrating the knowledge they've gained.

SUMMARY

The purpose of this chapter is to describe several instructional strategies as they relate to technology integration. Various strategies were discussed in terms of the balancing act in the point of tension between the teacher-directed and student-centered approach as it relates to technology integration. While each teacher will most likely make instructional decisions based upon their personal ideas of learning, it is important to understand that all instructional decisions, especially those detailed above, have implications for both the student and the teacher.

By adding more structure and taking more control away, students will not be as responsible for their learning, but then they will probably not need as much support to complete the learning tasks. For example, when integrating technology from a very structured instructional approach the teacher might: (a) define group roles and tasks and outlines the activity; (b) require specific technology tool(s) for students to collect, organize, analyze, and share their findings in a very specific manner; and (c) provide templates that students follow to create all of their technology-produced artifacts.

However, since students would not be responsible for planning, structuring, and designing their meaningful products, they will also miss discussing and deciding upon their team's organization and the technology tools they would use to gather, organize, or analyze their data. In addition, they will also miss the opportunity to think about their learning and how they might use a technology tool that best supports constructing new ideas and concepts as they construct a meaningful product that will best represent their findings.

By providing less structure, students will have to take more responsibility for their learning in terms of having to: (a) identify and organize group roles, tasks, and outlines of the activity; (b) select specific technology tool(s) to collect, organize, and analyze data; and (c) identify, learn, and utilize technology tools to help them produce artifacts that demonstrate their newly constructed knowledge, which, in turn, gives them greater control over the many aspects of learning.

This approach will require teachers to provide more soft scaffolds, such as individual tutoring, mini lessons, and individualized resources. Teachers will also need to provide support by acting as partners in the learning process alongside the students—perhaps even playing other roles such as instructor, trainer, coach, and tutor. However, while playing these roles the teacher can pose thought-provoking questions to help encourage critical thinking by students about how to create a meaningful product that best represents their findings, and advise them on what things they would need to tell the audience about their findings to get their story across.

As one can see, there are various ways a teacher might approach teaching and integrate technology and various instructional strategies. However, it is important to remember that the teacher's decisions can profoundly impact his or her students' learning experience. When thinking about integrating technology within some of these instructional strategies in the classroom, the teacher must consider some the elements. What is his or her comfort level— in terms of the *point of tension* between being responsible for students' learning and giving them the opportunity to take control and responsibility for their learning? What types of scaffolds, support, and resources might the teacher need to provide his or her students, in terms of requisite background knowledge, group work, organizing, and managing their learning and technology skills? Finally, but most importantly, how can teachers best serve their students' learning needs?

REFERENCES

Ertmer, P. A. and Simons, K. D. (2006). Jumping the PBL implementation hurdle: Supporting the efforts of K–12 teachers. *The Interdisciplinary Journal of Problem-based Learning, 1* (1), 40–54.

Matthews, R. S., Cooper, J. L., Davidson, N. and Hawkes, P. (1995). Building bridges between cooperative and collaborative learning. *Change* 27, 34–40.

Palincsar, A. S. (1986). *Reciprocal teaching. In Teaching reading as thinking.* Oak Brook, IL: North Central Regional Educational Laboratory.

Panitz, T. (1996). A definition of collaborative versus cooperative learning. *Deliberations* [Online]. Available: http://www.londonmet.ac.uk/deliberations/collaborative-learning/panitz-paper.cfm.

Roschelle, J., and Teasley, S. (1995). The construction of shared knowledge in collaborative problem solving. In C. E. O'Malley (ed.), *Computer supported collaborative learning* (pp. 69–197). Berlin Heidelberg, New York: Springer.

Roseth, C. J., Garfield, J. B., and Ben-Zvi, D. (2008). Collaboration in learning and teaching statistics. *Journal of Statistics Education, 16* (1) [Online]. Available: http://www.amstat.org/publications/jse/v16n1/roseth.html.

Savery, J. R. (2006). Overview of problem-based learning: Definitions and distinctions. *The Interdisciplinary Journal of Problem-based Learning, 1* (1), 9–20.

Saye J. W., and Brush, T. (2002). Scaffolding critical reasoning about history and social issues in multimedia-supported learning environments. *Educational Technology Research and Development, 50* (3), 77–96.

Slavin, R. E. (1997). *Educational psychology: Theory and practice* (fifth ed.). Needham Heights, MA: Allyn & Bacon.

Wood, D., Bruner, J., and Ross, G. (1974). The role of tutoring in problem solving. *Journal of Child Psychology and Psychiatry, 17,* 89–100.

Chapter 3

Standards and Assessment

Prior to the educational standards–based movement, teachers decided what their students would learn, which was generally based on agreed-upon district grades and discipline curriculum. Beginning in the late 1980s, academic standards were identified to provide standardized outcomes that students would know of and be able to achieve in the various disciplines at specific grade levels, regardless of district or teacher. Adopting specific discipline and grade-level standards was seen as a way to ensure that students would achieve the identified outcomes of those standards.

This chapter will provide a brief overview of current national standards and focus on how teachers might assess student achievement of academic standards based upon the digital artifacts that they create. As such, it is important to remember that this chapter will not provide details on all aspects of assessment. There are textbooks devoted entirely to the topic of assessment. These should be considered for a more in-depth analysis on the topic.

ACADEMIC STANDARDS

While one might imagine that standards would be "standardized," and indeed, there are quite a few national and international organizations, including the US government and even state governments that have identified academic standards. This has become a very politically charged topic. While various educational standards might be similar, designing them begs several questions. What knowledge, skills, and understandings should our children have? Who should decide those? How will we know if our students have achieved them? What can be done if they don't?

The biggest change in the standards-based education reform happened in 2002, when the No Child Left Behind (NCLB) legislation (Elementary and Secondary Education Act, 2015) was enacted nationally. NCLB combined the notion of having academic standards that defined what our children should know and required state-designed assessments to provide accountability, with penalties for schools that did not meet the prescribed levels of success.

To fulfill NCLB, states defined state educational standards, often derived from the discipline standards, but also created an assessment that would then be aligned to the states' standards. Therefore, since each state was in the process of developing their own assessment methods, many then developed their own standards, which would be aligned directly to the assessment test.

The process of designing standards and assessments is quite complex. Once standards have been defined, achievement outcomes need to be listed and then *performance indicators* for those outcomes need to be identified to ensure that students have achieved those standards. Next, teachers need to become familiar with and understand the standards and performance indicators for which they are responsible. Then an assessment must be developed that accurately and reliably measures how well a student has achieved the performance indicators.

Not all state departments of education agree on what the standards should be, nor on how their students might be assessed. Each state's standards and assessments can be different. One of the biggest challenges of creating academic standards has been agreeing on outcomes that are appropriate for the various grade levels for each of the specific disciplines.

Teachers need to know their state's standards for their grade level and discipline, as students are assessed and need to be ready to take the test their state requires. To help prepare students, teachers should embed the performance objectives of the various standards in their lessons. This is generally done by breaking down the standards and then designing lessons and units that will help them learn and achieve the performance indicators within those standards. This can be a bit confusing, but here is a simpler way to think about it. Of course a lot of details must be filled in, but it really boils down to these three questions:

1. *What do teachers want their students to learn?* Teachers must decide what they want their students to achieve. That is, they should identify the performance indicators within the specific standard they plan on teaching.
2. *How will teachers help students learn that?* Teachers must decide how they are going to help their students achieve that. They must identify and plan the lesson so that it will help their students achieve that performance indicator (e.g., they need to decide what instructional methods or strategies they will employ and identify what materials, technologies, or other resources students will use to help them learn).

3. *How will teachers know how much the students have learned?* Teachers must decide how they are going to know if their students have met the performance indicator. They need to plan assessments of their students' achievement of the outcomes accurately and reliably.

National Academic Organizations

Over the years, each discipline has since revised and realigned their standards, which were then adopted or revised by states for their own state standards. Here are a few examples.

To begin with, the National Council of Teachers of Mathematics (NCTM) wrote their national standards for mathematics in 1989, but these standards have since been revised. Currently, the "NCTM Principles and Standards" acts as a guide to educators for the continued improvement of mathematics education (National Council for the Teachers of Mathematics, 2015).

The "Standards for the English Language Arts" (ELA) was originally published by the National Council of Teachers of English (NCTE) and the International Reading Association (IRA) in 1996 and designed to complement other national, state, and local standards. They were reaffirmed by the NCTE Executive Committee in November 2012 and are currently available on their website (National Council of Teachers of English, 2015).

The National Council for Social Studies first released the "Curriculum Standards for Social Studies: Expectations of Excellence" in 1994. This was revised and the "National Curriculum Standards for Social Studies: A Framework for Teaching, Learning, and Assessment" was enhanced in 2013 through the efforts of fifteen organizations that collaborated to provide guidance to deepen instruction in civics, economics, geography, and history at the K–12 level. The "College, Career and Civic Life (C3) Framework for Social Studies State Standards" (NCSS, 2013) details four dimensions to better support teachers of social studies.

"The National Science Education Standards" were developed by a wide body of governmental, educational, and public groups and individuals (National Academies Press, 1996, p. 106). In addition, in 2013, "The Next Generation Science Standards" (NGSS) were released and included partners such as: National Research Council, National Science Teachers Association, American Association for the Advancement of Science, and Achieve—an independent education reform organization (Achieve, Inc., 2015).

Common Core State Standards Initiative

In 2010, the National Governors Association Center for Best Practices (NGA) and the Council of Chief State School Officers (CCSSO) published the "Common Core (CC) Standards" (Common Core State Standards Initiative,

2015) to help better standardize and introduce some common student out-comes that all could agree on. In addition, review and feedback during the development of the Common Core was provided by the National Education Association (NEA), American Federation of Teachers (AFT), NCTM, and NCTE, among other organizations.

The "Common Core Standards" focus on an integrated model of literacy, suggesting that students should be able to read, write, speak, and listen in English and language arts, which will help them achieve literacy in history/social studies, science, and technical subjects. To help delineate between grade levels, the standards are organized into two sections; K–8 and 9–12.

Common Core ELA

The Common Core ELA (CCELA) Standards focuses on English, language arts, and literacy in history/social studies, science, and technical subjects. There are four key features of the CCELA:

- Reading: text complexity and the growth of comprehension
- Writing: text types, responding do reading, and research
- Speaking and listening: flexible communication and collaboration
- Language: conventions, effective use, and vocabulary

Reading is then broken down into three types: foundational skills, litera-ture, and informational text. The foundational skills category has four subcat-egories: (a) print concepts, (b) phonological awareness, (c) phonics and word recognition, and (d) fluency. Both literature and informational text have four subcategories: (a) key ideas and details, (b) craft and structure, (c) integration of knowledge and ideas, and (d) range of reading and level of text complexity.

In addition, each category has grade-level descriptors. For example, fourth-grade students should attain *fluency* in *foundational skills* by being able to "Read with sufficient accuracy and fluency to support comprehension; (a) Read grade-level text with purpose and understanding. (b) Read grade-level prose and poetry orally with accuracy, appropriate rate, and expression on successive readings. (c) Use context to confirm or self-correct word recogni-tion and understanding, rereading as necessary" (Common Core State Stan-dards Initiative, 2015, p. 17).

Common Core Mathematics

The Common Core Mathematics Standards takes a less integrated approach, but was also designed to help make the standards and curriculum coherent, as Schmidt, Houang, and Cogan (2002) stated, "by stressing conceptual understanding of key ideas, but also by continually returning to organizing principles such as place value or the properties of operations to structure those ideas" (p. 4).

There are two types of Common Core Mathematics Standards, one is the Standards for Mathematical Practice and the other is the Standards for Mathematical Content. According to the mathematical practice standards, students should be able to do the following:

1. Make sense of problems and persevere in solving them.
2. Reason abstractly and quantitatively.
3. Construct viable arguments and critique the reasoning of others.
4. Model with mathematics.
5. Use appropriate tools strategically.
6. Attend to precision.
7. Look for and make use of structure.
8. Look for and express regularity in repeated reasoning.

Each grade level then has its specific content standards that build upon prior grade-level learning. For example, "In Grade 2, instructional time should focus on four critical areas: (1) extending understanding of base-ten notation; (2) building fluency with addition and subtraction; (3) using standard units of measure; and (4) describing and analyzing shapes" (p. 17).

Issues with Common Core

Each state was given the choice of adopting the "Common Core Standards" and initially, forty-five states adopted the CC. While this book is being written, however, some state departments of education are choosing to "rebrand" or move away from the Common Core completely. Some have concerns regarding the national government taking control of local school curriculum. However, many other state departments of education cite a huge concern over the online assessment costs developed by vendors such as the Partnership for Assessment of Readiness for College and Careers (PARCC) consortium (Rix, 2013).

While the future of the Common Core is unclear, they are an initial attempt to provide a *common* set of K–12 outcomes in English, language arts, literacy, and mathematics for college and career-ready standards (Bidwell, 2014). Indeed, even the No Child Left Behind campaign is being reconsidered (Elementary and Secondary Act, 2015).

National Educational Technology Standards

There are also technology standards developed by the International Society for Technology in Education (ISTE). As of 2007, they were renamed the National Educational Technology Standards (NETS), labeling them

Standards*S for students, Standards*T for teachers, Standards*A for school administrators, Standards*C for technology coaches to help support peers becoming digital educators, and Standards*CSE for computer science educators. The student standards help teachers think about technology outcomes for students, and teacher standards provide outcomes for technology integration.

USING DIGITAL TOOLS FOR ASSESSMENT

While the standards that students encounter may vary, depending upon state, every classroom teacher will be responsible in helping his or her students meet some performance indicators. Once identified, instructional and lesson planning can begin. In addition, assessment must be planned to find out what students have achieved or learned. Having students create digital products for assessment can make this a bit more complex. To add to this, there are two types of assessments that should be employed: summative assessments and formative assessments.

Summative Assessments

A summative assessment acts as a summation report *of* learning and is designed to assess the student's achievement generally at the end of a lesson, unit, or even a grade level. The summative assessment should accurately measure the student's achievement of the targeted performance indicators. A quality summative assessment should be designed that provides assessment information to the teacher, the students, and others.

There are a variety of ways by which this can be done. The key is keeping in mind the term alignment, meaning that the assessment should *accurately* assess the students to see if they've achieved the performance indicators. While this might seem pretty straightforward, it is easy to lose track when looking at the digital products students create, like a slide show presentation.

Chappuis et al. (2012) describe keys to quality assessment:

1. They are designed to serve the *specific needs of intended user(s).*
2. They are based on clearly articulated and appropriate *achievement targets.*
3. They *accurately measure* student achievement.
4. They yield results that are *effectively communicated* to the intended users.
5. They *involve students* in self-assessment, goal setting, tracking, reflecting on, and sharing their learning (p. 3).

This can be further elaborated. First, an assessment should provide specific and detailed information for a variety of people, including teachers, their students, the students' parents, and the administration. When thinking about designing an assessment it is important to know who will be using the information gained.

Second, the assessment should have *clear targets*, which can also be defined as the performance indicators outlined in the standards discussed in the previous section. When thinking about designing an assessment being *aligned* to the identified performance indicators for the lesson is key.

Third, the assessment should be well designed, in terms of the criteria accurately matched to the performance indicators. The assessment should be appropriate for the learning task and grade level and should not be biased or impacted by another variable.

Fourth, effective communication should provide feedback to intended users on a variety of levels; it should guide instruction for the teacher and provide feedback to the student for the future. Achievement levels should be tracked and communicated or reported and should accurately indicate achievement.

Fifth, students should be involved in the assessment. In other words, the assessment should provide helpful information to the students. They should be clearly aware of the assessment criteria and/or performance indicators. The assessments should allow them to keep track of progress and use the information to reflect upon and set their own learning goals.

Formative Assessments

A question that is often asked of new teachers is: *"What would you do if you designed and taught a unit, then gave an end of the unit test and all of your students failed?"* While it could be possible that all of the students failed, the point to consider here is why? The problem could have been with the lesson design, the teaching of the lesson, or the assessment. To keep this from happening, teachers often use *formative assessments* to keep track of the learning progress during the unit, thus reducing the possibility of that happening.

Formative assessments have the specific purpose of improving or enhancing learning by clearly communicating relevant information on each student's progress. Formative assessments can also inform teachers on how well the lesson was designed and/or how well it is being taught, that is, it can provide information on the clarity of a lesson, the efficacy of an instructional strategy, and whether there has been sufficient practice of complex skills. In other words, a good formative assessment can provide information during the lesson on the students' progress that will help improve the learning environment enhancing their opportunity to better achieve the objectives.

ASSESSMENT EXAMPLE

Juanita, a second-grade teacher, has designed a lesson that she wants to teach to help her students meet the Next Generation Science Standards (NGSS: 2-LS2-1). The performance indicator states that students should be able to *plan and conduct an investigation to determine if plants need sunlight and water to grow.* This standard includes the disciplinary core ideas that there is an interdependent relationships in ecosystems (LS2.A), that is, that *plants depend on water and light to grow* (2-LS2-1) and including the NGSS Cross-cutting Concept of Cause and Effect where *events have causes that generate observable patterns* (2-LS2-1) (Achieve, 2015).

Juanita decides that students will work in teams planting beans and provide differing amounts of sunlight and water to help them see how these elements impact plant growth. As the students begin to think about the task, they decide that some teams would give their plant different amounts of water while other teams would give their plants different amounts of sunlight by keeping them in the classroom closet and moving them to the window. They would use a ruler to measure how high the plants grew and also take pictures of the plants as they grew.

As a formative assessment, Juanita takes anecdotal notes of the students' plans to help gain an understanding of their ability to "*plan* an investigation to determine if plants need sunlight and water to grow." Students will record all experiment data into a project log. Juanita also collects and reviews each student's log to assess ability to "*conduct* an investigation to determine if plants need sunlight and water to grow."

As a summative assessment, Juanita decides that she would have each team create a research report to assess if they had learned that "*plants need water and light to grow*" and what happened when either *water* or *light* was not provided (i.e., cause and effect). The research report would be a presentation that included their pictures and each student would record their own concluding remarks. While the presentation can then serve as the summative assessment product, it is important to design a good assessment instrument, and she considers the five keys to a quality assessment.

To meet the first key the rubric needs to have details that will help everyone understand how it will *serve the needs of the teacher and his or her students.* To meet the second key, the rubric needs to *clearly articulate the appropriate achievement indicators.* An easy way to do this is to copy and paste the specific standard indicator into the criteria row, so it will be directly aligned.

To meet the third key, the rubric needs to have appropriate descriptors to *accurately measure* various levels of achievement. A rubric generally includes three or four levels of achievement and for each criteria row, there should be appropriate descriptors. To meet the fourth key, the rubric needs to be clear and shared with students prior to their engaging in the unit so that the expectations will be *effectively communicated*. To meet the fifth key, the rubric needs to *involve students*. In this case, by having students share their movies, they can reflect upon their team's presentation and their learning.

Juanita wants to assess three things. First, her students' achievements of being able to plan and conduct an investigation to determine if plants need sunlight and water to grow; second, the disciplinary core ideas of understanding that plants depend on water and light to grow; and third, to see whether the cause of not receiving sufficient of either has an effect. To do so, her rubric should include specific details on the criteria of meeting those elements. The individual concluding remarks by each student in the final research report should include: (1) a statement that plants depend upon water and sunlight to grow, and (2) a description of what happened to plants that did not receive appropriate amounts of either water or sunlight (i.e., a discussion of cause and effect).

She also wants to consider technical criteria for the presentation. While not essential for measuring the outcomes of the science standard, her students will want to know what she expects. She decided on the following criteria: (1) four to five slides, (2) a title with author names, (3) images that demonstrate growth or lack of growth, (4) a table of the amount of water provided and the corresponding dates, (5) a table of the amount of sunlight provided and the corresponding dates, (6) age-appropriate grammar and spelling for any text, and (7) concluding remarks.

Collaborative, Team, and Individual Assessments

Because Juanita has her students working in teams, she needs to decide how to assess each student's individual achievement. Although the research report presentation might score very well according to the assessment rubric, it's important for her to know the level of achievement of every individual team member.

Cooperative learning has been researched for years with consistent findings (Slavin, 1990) and suggests that *positive interdependence* between team members (i.e., having group goals) and *individual accountability* provide the structure that supports enhanced student achievement and methods for individual assessment.

To provide for individual accountability and then individual summative assessment, Juanita will assess each student for their concluding remarks. See table 3.1, which illustrates the criteria for the *individual content rubric* to score the content for each student's concluding remarks. This provides an individual summative assessment for the outcomes of the unit.

Table 3.1 Individual Content Assessment Rubric

Criteria	Approaches 0–69%	Meets 70–89%	Exceeds 90–100%	Score
Examples of data on the impacts of human activities causing the identified pollution.	There was at least one accurate example that included the quantities and types of pollutants released. Examples although accurate were limited in details on changes and didn't include elements of biomass, species diversity, and/or areal changes in land surface use. Examples, although accurate, were limited regarding urban development, agriculture, livestock, and/or surface mining.	There were multiple examples with some details of the quantities and types of pollutants released. Examples included details on changes to biomass or species diversity, or areal changes in land surface use. Examples included urban development, agriculture, livestock, and/or surface mining.	There were multiple accurate examples that detailed the quantities and types of pollutants released. Examples provided accurate details on changes to biomass and species diversity, and areal changes in land surface use. Examples included accurate details on urban development, agriculture, livestock, and/or surface mining.	
Examples for limiting future impacts of the identified pollutants from local efforts.	The presentation included at least one accurate example of one of the three R's of limited resources: • Reducing, • Reusing, and • Recycling	The presentation included at least one accurate example of each of the three R's of limited resources: • Reducing, • Reusing, and • Recycling	The presentation included multiple accurate examples of each of the three R's of limited resources: • Reducing, • Reusing, and • Recycling	
Examples of large-scale geoengineering design solutions.	The movie included at least one accurate example of altering global temperatures by making big changes to the atmosphere, ocean, or land.	The movie included at least one accurate example of altering global temperatures by making big changes to the atmosphere, ocean, and land.	The movie included multiple accurate examples of altering global temperatures by making big changes to the atmosphere, ocean, and land.	

Table 3.2   Team Checklist

Technical Criteria	10–9	8	7	6–0	Weight	Score
4–5 slides					1	
Title with author names					1	
Images that demonstrate growth					1.5	
Table of dates and amounts of water provided					1.5	
Table of dates and amounts of sunlight provided					1.5	
Age-appropriate grammar and spelling for any text					1	
Each student's individual concluding remarks					2	

Juanita will use a *team checklist,* to provide a score to assess the technical criteria (see table 3.2). This score becomes a *team score* for the research report presentation, which is given to each team member. Having a team score provides a common goal and supports positive interdependence of students working together to do the best they can—as a team.

Providing Structure

This activity is somewhat complex, especially for second graders and it might be necessary to give students more structure for a project-based learning unit such as this. Providing step-by-step guidance where students use digital tools to create products can help them successfully complete the final product. In addition to helping them stay on track through the complex learning tasks, each digital product the students create can serve as formative assessments to help identify who might need additional individual help, support, and/or scaffolds.

As students go through each step of the project, observations, files, and records can serve as formative assessment data to help maintain an understanding of how well the students are doing and when and what they need help on at any time during the process.

Team Roles and Tasks

Many students at this age need help in organizing a team, planning steps, identifying tasks, and assigning roles that include very specific tasks. It is also a good idea for the teacher to meet with each group of students assigned the same role to help them understand their specific task for that role. In addition, it gives the teacher the opportunity to impart additional instruction, but also helps develop a peer support group should they forget how to perform their task.

In teams of three, one student becomes the team leader, one becomes the record keeper, and one becomes the photographer. The team leader would help make sure that the other two students do their task accurately, that is, knowing how much water and sunlight their plants would get. The record keeper keeps track by measuring the plant's growth and recording how much water and sunlight the plant gets. The photographer uses a digital camera or smartphone to take pictures each day the plants are measured and saves images in a storage area for later use.

Using a Planning Tool

One way to help students think about what they know and how they might organize a science experiment is to have them use a cognitive mapping tool. One such tool is Kidspiration (2016), which can be projected so that the class can think about and add items as they discuss the project while the teacher engages the students in a discussion with questions like: Why do you think that plants need to grow? What do you think would happen if they didn't get those things? Using Kidspiration, their ideas can be organized into a cognitive map that will help them organize their experiment.

Using a Data Recording Tool (Google Forms)

Google Forms is a great digital tool to help students record their experiment data. Using a teacher-created Google Form, students can record their daily data on the amount of water provided, the hours of sunlight, and plant growth. Once entered into the Google Form, the data is then available for review in a Google spreadsheet and a click on the "Response Summary" generates charts and graphs based on the data. By discussing the results with the help of these graphic representations, students can better understand what the numbers might mean.

File Saving

When organizing a project-based learning unit, such as this, it's important that students have easy-to-use storage space. Some districts or schools provide students digital storage areas. If not, Dropbox (2016) is an easy-to-use online storage area that many teachers use for this type of file organization. Students can upload the digital files into their team's project folder.

SUMMARY

This chapter provided an overview of various academic standards and how digital tools can be integrated to help provide assessments of the performance indicators outlined in the standards. Examples were provided that detailed how student achievement of those performance indicators might be assessed, both in a formative and summative manner by looking at student products created using digital tools. It is important to note that assessment is a very complex topic and the purpose of this chapter was not to cover it completely.

However, the examples provided should be seen as models for assessing achievement of standards-based performance indicators using meaningful products that students create using digital tools. Integrating technology in a project-based or problem-based learning method where students conduct inquiry, investigation, and practice can be quite complex and require a great deal of planning, structure, and scaffolding. It is hoped that the reader will gain a better idea of how that might be done by integrating digital tools that can help learners accomplish this task.

REFERENCES AND RESOURCES

Achieve, Inc. (2015a). *Next Generation Science Standards: For States, By States. (NGSS).* Retrieved from: http://www.nextgenscience.org/next-generation-science-standards.

Achieve, Inc. (2015b). *Next Generation Science Standards: For States, By States. (NGSS).* HS-ESS3–6: Human Sustainability. Retrieved from: http://www.nextgen-science.org/hsess-hs-human-sustainability.

Bidwell, A. (2014). *Common core in free fall.* U.S. News & World Report. Retrieved from: http://www.usnews.com/news/articles/2014/08/20/common-core-support-waning-most-now-oppose-standards-national-surveys-show.

Chappuis, J., Stiggins, R., Chappuis, S., and Arter, J. (2012). *Classroom assessment for student learning: Doing it right—using it well.* Upper Saddle River, NJ: Pearson Education, Inc. ISBN: 978-0-13-26588-7.

Common Core State Standards Initiative: Preparing America's students for college and career. (2015). *Read the standards.* Retrieved from: http://www.corestandards.org/read-the-standards.

Dropbox. (2016). Dropbox works the way you do. Retrieved from: https://www.dropbox.com/.

Elementary and Secondary Education Act. (2015). Retrieved from: http://www.ed.gov/esea.

Google. (2015). Google Forms. Retrieved from: https://www.google.com/forms/about/.

International Society for Technology in Education (ISTE). (2008). *Standards.* Retrieved from: http://www.iste.org/standards/iste-standards/standards-for-teachers.

Inspiration Software, Inc. (2015). Kidspiration—The visual way to explore understand words, numbers and concepts. Retrieved from: http://www.inspiration.com/Kidspiration.

National Academies Press. (1996). National Science Education Standards (NSES). Retrieved from: http://www.nap.edu/openbook.php?record_id=4962.

National Council for Social Studies. (NCSS). (2010). National curriculum standards for social studies: A framework for teaching, learning and assessment. Retrieved from: http://www.socialstudies.org/standards.

National Council for the Social Studies. (NCSS). (2013). The College, Career, and Civic Life (C3) Framework for Social Studies State Standards: Guidance for Enhancing Rigor of K–12 Civics, Economics, Geography and History. Silver Spring, MD: NCSS.

National Council of Teachers of English (NCTE) and the International Reading Association (IRA). (2015). Standards for the English language arts. Retrieved from: http://www.ncte.org/standards/ncte-ira.

National Council of Teachers of Mathematics. (NCTM). (2015). *Principles and standards.* Retrieved from: http://www.nctm.org/Standards-and-Positions/Principles-and-Standards/.

Rix, K. (2013). *Common core under attack.* Scholastic, Inc. Retrieved from: http://www.scholastic.com/browse/article.jsp?id=3758244.

Schmidt, W., Houang, R., and Cogan, L. (Summer 2002). "A Coherent Curriculum: The Case of Mathematics," *American Educator*, p. 4.

Slavin, R. E. (1990). Research on cooperative learning: Consensus and controversy. *Educational Leadership*, 47 (4), 52–54.

Part II

DIGITAL TOOLS FOR LEARNING

Each chapter in Part II discusses digital tools that can support and assist elementary student learning. In addition, this part provides contextually based elementary classroom examples that illustrate each chapters' technology concepts. Every chapter also includes a scenario that analyzes integrating the digital tools discussed in those chapters to help students meet national standards and achieve specific, elementary-grade-level objectives/outcomes.

Chapter 4

Technology Operations

Because technology changes at such a rapid rate, to fully support students, teachers should have a good understanding of basic computer functions. This chapter will focus on vital computer concepts that can be compared and contrasted to human information processing. It is hoped that comparing the similarities between human information processes and computer processes will provide a metaphor upon which to build a better understanding.

HUMANS AND COMPUTERS

Computer hardware and operating systems (OSs) can be a bit complex or confusing and some people have difficulties understanding how a computer actually works. Often, however, computer processing concepts are explained in terms of human brain functions, particularly memory. This comparison may provide a scaffold upon which to better gain an understanding of technology processes.

Human Information Processing: Multi-store Memory Model

Most humans *process information* as defined in the Multi-Store Model (Atkinson and Shiffrin, 1968). As shown in figure 4.1, a person first hears, sees, or perhaps feels something, experiencing some kind of environmental input that goes into the sensory information store. *Attention* is then focused on the sensory input and the brain begins to *process* the information received in short-term memory, also known as working memory.

Next, the person *thinks* about how this information relates to what he or she already knows, comparing and contrasting it to prior knowledge in terms of

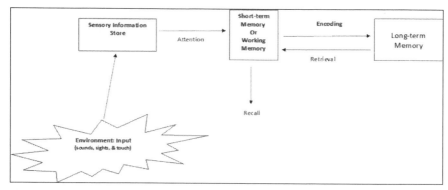

Figure 4.1   The Basic Structure and Processes of the Atkinson and Shiffrin Multi-Store Model

information and experiences held in long-term memory. If the information is new it is encoded and sent to long-term memory to be available in the future.

If the new information is very complex, however, one might have to retrieve and encode it back and forth several times with past experiences and background knowledge to better understand that sensory input. As one is engaged (paying attention) he or she *processes* the information to the point where it makes sense and builds new or enhances existing knowledge.

Computer Information Processing

Computers work in a similar fashion, as shown in figure 4.2. When the computer is turned on, *basic input/output system* (BIOS) is activated. The BIOS is imprinted on the computer *motherboard*, which is the main circuit board that connects all the computer parts. When the BIOS is activated, it provides basic information regarding what hardware is connected to the motherboard and, most importantly, instructs the computer to look for and start the *operating system* (OS), which is either Windows, Macintosh, or Linux.

The computer OS, for example Windows, is really just software that is most often stored on the hard drive and is configured in a manner that helps all of the other hardware and peripherals (RAM, hard drive, monitor, mouse, printer, scanner, etc.) function properly. For example, the OS helps the monitor display what users need to see, the mouse to move to select items, and the keyboard to enter text to use the computer.

Computer functions can be compared with the sensory information store in human information processing, the element that receives input. In the case of the computer, however, the OS is a software that sets up communication channels between the various parts and waits for information from the input

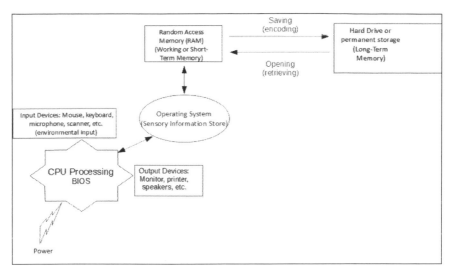

Figure 4.2   Structure and Processes of the Computer

devices (i.e., mouse, keyboard, etc.). Simply put, the OS helps all the computer parts function with one another.

As *input* devices create information (i.e., using a mouse to select an item or using a keyboard to type), the OS receives, organizes, and directs that information to the central processing unit (CPU) to be *processed*. The CPU processing the information could be compared to a person paying attention or thinking about something. This is similar to how one *processes* things seen, heard, or read and then leaving it to the brain to decide what to do with that information.

In the computer, the OS and the CPU work together to help it make sense of all of the information that moves around and through it. All this happens within the computer's RAM. The RAM is where the computer thinks about all of the information while *working on something*. The RAM is much like short-term memory in humans because it is a working area where the computer can temporarily store and work with information. When using a word processor to write a paper, the key strokes create text on the page, which is held in the computer's RAM.

Information held in the computer's RAM is not kept permanently and must be saved to the hard drive or some other storage device, much like humans encoding information to long-term memory. This is why if a computer is shut down before work is saved, the work is often lost; RAM is *temporary*. However, if saved to the hard drive or other permanent storage places, information can be retrieved to be viewed or edited at a later date.

When information or processes are complex the computer may function much like human encoding by retrieving complex data back and forth between long-term and short-term memory. For example, while typing a paper, current word processors can recognize that the user typed a word incorrectly and then retrieves the correct spelling to automatically apply it to the word. The incorrect spelling is only held in RAM, while the correct spelling is stored on the hard drive but the word processor and OS work together to move information back and forth to fix the misspelling.

Since people need to be able to see what input they are providing (i.e., through typing or mouse movements), the computer also has *output* devices. The most common is the computer screen. However, there are other output devices, such as printers and speakers. For example, once a paper is written it can be sent to the printer for a hard copy.

SOFTWARE, FILE STORAGE, AND FILE MANAGEMENT

As mentioned above, the OS is the software that organizes and manages the computer. In addition, there are other software applications designed to perform specific tasks and functions. Microsoft Office and LibreOffice include word processing, presentation, and spreadsheet software that are considered productivity tools. These could also be called computer-based software and are often installed on computers upon purchase. Alternatively, they could also be bought and installed on a later date.

Some software, such as Google Docs, are not really installed on the computer but can be accessed via the Internet. For example, the Chromebook doesn't have any software installed on the computer for the most part. To use it for most any type of word processing, users must be connected to the Internet so they can use the server-based software, Google Docs (Google, 2015). The big difference here is understanding where the software resides, on the computer or on the Internet.

Computer-Based Software

New computers often have quite a bit of software already installed on the hard drive, such as productivity tools, an Internet browser, an email client, among others. Software designed for specific functions can also be purchased and installed on the hard drive. Some of these can be very expensive, but there are also open-source software applications that can be downloaded and installed, generally for free. These serve the same purpose as the very expensive software. The key is that if it is installed on the computer, it can generally be used offline.

Server-Based Software

There are also available software applications that do not reside in a computer. Many of these are free. Google Docs is a good example of server-based software and could be described as the Google Cloud. Google Docs isn't installed on a computer, but rather is accessed via the Internet. Google accounts are free and permit the creation of all kinds of productivity documents similar to, *and most importantly compatible with*, Microsoft Office, that is, word processing, presentations, spreadsheets, and others.

Files created in Google Docs are saved online as well. However, they can also be uploaded and downloaded to and from a computer hard drive as well. Google Docs is only one example of the many software applications that are server-based, meaning that they don't reside on the computer and therefore cannot be accessed without being online. Indeed, Microsoft's OneDrive (2015) is comparable to Google Docs. The key here is that one cannot use this type of software without Internet access.

Open-Source Software

Although available for several decades, many folks are not aware of or familiar with open-source software. The Open Source Initiative (2015) supports computer-based software, which can be downloaded and installed for free. For example, Ubuntu is a free Linux Distribution OS with the philosophy "that software should be free and accessible to all" (Canonical Ltd., 2015, para 1.).

Developed, delivered, and supported by the Ubuntu community, this OS includes additional software such as Firefox web browser (Mozilla, 2015a) and Thunderbird email client (Mozilla, 2015b). In addition, Ubuntu includes LibreOffice, a productivity tool that parallels Microsoft Office and allows users to open, edit, and then save word documents, spreadsheets, presentations, and others created in Microsoft Office.

LibreOffice (The Document Team, 2015) can also be downloaded and installed onto computers running Apple's Macintosh or Microsoft's Windows OSs. In other words, one does not need to be running the Linux OS to take advantage of open-source software. Other software titles such as Audacity (2015), a free audio recording and editing software, and Gimp (2015), an image editing software that parallels Photoshop (Acrobat), are also available and can be downloaded for free and installed on Linux, Windows, and Macintosh OSs.

Being knowledgeable about open-source software can be a huge advantage for teachers to provide their students with technology tools, especially when their schools or districts don't have the financial resources to purchase some of the very expensive software.

File or Data Storage

When a file is saved, it is saved in the form of a data file in a *storage* area. If the software being used is computer-based, it is generally saved on the computer's hard drive. When saving a file using server-based software, however, it is generally saved on the server where the software resides. Sometimes this can be autosaved, meaning that the server software automatically saves as a person continues working.

Data storage is often compared to a filing cabinet because work or data files are like pieces of paper that can be organized into folders and subfolders. Generally, a computer OS creates some standard folders for specific kinds of files to help one organize data. There are usually folders called Documents, Pictures, Music, Movies, and/or Videos.

While this is a good way to get started in keeping files organized, it can get more complicated when working in a school computer lab, as there are many other options for storage. It is important to understand some of the more complex aspects of data storage and file management to be able to find work in school or other public computer labs.

Local Storage

Local storage is often a term that is used for a computer's hard drive because it is the storage device that is located on the local computer where files can be stored. When writing a paper on a home computer, for example, it will most likely be saved on the computer's hard drive. This works well if one is using a specific computer. However, if working on a shared computer in a school lab or at a friend's house, files should be saved on *removable* or *network storage*.

Removable Storage

Removable storage is often a good place to save work when working on shared computers or computers at different locations. There are many types of removable storage devices currently available to connect to just about any type of computer. Removable or portable USB storage devices come in two basic types and can be a very inexpensive option and compatible with just about any computer.

One type is called a portable hard drive. These are usually about the size of a small book, but can hold a lot of data. This type of portable drive might be good for a classroom teacher who wants to keep a lot of data in one location.

Other types called "thumb," "flash," or "USB" drives are very small, but can still hold a substantial amount of files or data.

Both portable hard drives and thumb or flash drives are generally good for individual students and can be simply plugged into the USB port on the computer. This allows the student to carry his or her files at all times from one working location to another. The downside is that a flash drive is so small that it is very easy to forget in the computer lab.

Network Storage (aka "The Cloud")

Network storage is another option for saving work in a school computer lab. This requires having access to a server where teachers and students can save work over the network. Most schools have a local area network (LAN), which is generally a small network that connects the local computers in the school or computer lab. The LAN is then connected to a wide area network (WAN), which is what provides Internet connectivity.

This type of network configuration provides greater security as it allows local computers to communicate with one another and get information to and from the Internet, as it doesn't let computers outside of the LAN (i.e., in the WAN) connect locally. A network storage area is often *mounted* (or linked) to the local computer so that when one saves a file, one simply locates and selects the appropriate *network drive*. Network storage can work very well in a school computer lab environment because students can access their personal storage area from any computer in the lab, school, or sometimes even from their homes.

The *cloud* or *cloud computing* are terms with which many are familiar. Actually, the cloud is really just network storage. The difference is that Microsoft, Apple, and many other companies have provided network storage on their servers, giving them special names such as iCloud. In addition, they have built-in applications into their OS to help automate the process of backing up music, photos, and other data files. This might be a good option, but one must be aware of where the backups are actually being saved and who might have access to them. While Google Docs doesn't really call their network storage a cloud, it could also be so considered.

File Management

Regardless of the type of storage one uses, it is important to organize files in some logical fashion. Perhaps one of the biggest difficulties people have when using a computer is not thinking about managing and organizing their files and just letting it happen haphazardly. It can be extremely frustrating and time consuming for students if they can't find the file they need.

There are endless ways to organize files, but it is very important for each person to find a way that works for him or her. Some organize their files by file types (i.e., all Word documents in one folder, all pictures in another folder, etc.), others organize their files by date (i.e., all files created in a certain period of time are stored in one folder), while still others organize their files by some relational structure (i.e., all files related to a course go into one folder, while files related to another course go into a different folder). It may take a little bit of time to organize one's files, but it is time well spent.

USERS WITH SPECIAL NEEDS

One of the most powerful aspects of a computer OS is that the input devices (mouse and keyboard) and output information (monitor and speakers) can be configured to support and better help users with special needs. All OSs (Macintosh, Windows, and Linux) have built-in tools that allow users to reconfigure the way information is received by the computer and then sent back to the user. Changing how the user controls the computer by using the mouse, keyboard, and/or microphone or by adjusting the way the monitor displays information can better support users with special needs.

To support the diverse needs of their students, teachers should be familiar with the equitable access tools to modify the way the computer receives or sends back information to better support students with impairments of vision, hearing, physical and motor skills, as well as learning and literacy. The accessibility tools on OSs are generally found in the control panel area where other computer configuration tools are located, and teachers in today's classrooms should be well versed in how to utilize these very helpful aspects of computer OSs to support their students with disabilities.

Specifically, Apple includes "Accessibility," which allows users to configure interactive elements within the computer. Accessibility provides support for students with various special needs on all Macintosh, iPhone, and iPad OSs. One example is a Voiceover Screen Reader tool for students with limited vision (Apple, 2015). Like the Apple iOS, Linux Distributions' Ubuntu and Linux Mint also label their accessibility tool, "Accessibility." It also allows users to configure the computer environment for those with various special needs. Windows OSs calls their accessibility tool "Ease of Access" (Microsoft, 2015).

Apple (2015) provides detailed instructions on how to adapt the Universal Access tools for the Macintosh. Microsoft (2015) also provides accessibility support. The Lasa Knowledgebase (Lasa Charity UK, Ltd., 2006) provides a good overview of accessibility on Linux-based computers.

TROUBLESHOOTING

Perhaps the best thing one can learn in terms of computers is to have a good bag of tricks for troubleshooting. Sometimes computer hardware is not configured properly or simply doesn't work, such as when your printer just won't print. It is at these times that we depend on the school technology gurus. However, they often simply go through a list of things that could be wrong, trying out options until things work again. It is this trial-and-error method that provides clues as to where the problem lies. Sometimes, if one simply tries out various options, the problem will work itself out.

If, on the other hand, one just can't figure it out and there is no one to call, a quick Internet search may provide the right answers. In addition to doing a quick Google search, there are many troubleshooting guides and help websites. For example, the Computer Hope (2016) website provides great basic computer troubleshooting support information.

SCENARIO: ORGANIZING AND SAVING FILES

Mary, a fourth-grade teacher, is designing an integrated unit where her students will be getting to know some of the outcomes of the Social Studies Standard I: Culture and the Social Studies Standard III: People, Places, and Environments (NCSS, 2015). She also wants the unit to help her students meet the objectives of Science Content Standard D: Earth and Space Science (National Academies Press, 1996), specifically weather. She wants them to become aware of and practice good data-saving habits. By doing so, she believes that she is teaching them to be more organized and, hence, less likely to lose their files, which might enhance their overall learning habits.

To help her students meet all of these outcomes she is designing a travel unit where students will work in teams to investigate specific vacation destinations and then create a multimedia presentation brochure that outlines information directly aligned to the social studies and science standards.

The students must include information regarding the language(s), folktales, music, and artistic creations of the culture of their assigned vacation destination (SS #1, Outcome C). They must also include a map, which demonstrates their understanding of the relative location, direction, size, and shape of the location (SS #3, Outcome A). Next, they must include information about the weather, that is, average temperature, average rainfall, and forecast for the time frame of the trip. Math standards could also be met by including other elements, such as travel costs (i.e., transportation, housing, food, etc.) and currency exchange rates.

Since Mary wants her students to demonstrate their technology skills, the brochure must include multimedia, (i.e., images, videos, audio narration, local music, etc.). However, Mary also knows that this unit will require students to assemble a lot of digital files. In addition to the presentation file, they will need to keep track of and organize the images, video, and audio files that they locate and download from the Internet.

She realized that lost or missing files was one of the major issues with this type of project in the past because of the way her computer lab was configured. While each teacher had classroom storage, students faced difficulty organizing and keeping their files separate from others. There were times when a student would overwrite another student's file because they both saved it using the same name and in the same location. Mary decided that she would try using some online tools to help her students organize their files and keep better track of them.

A quick search located an article titled "The 4 Best Cloud Storage Sites for Students" (Reviews.com, 2015). Two stuck out for her, Google Drive (2016) and Dropbox (2016). Both provided free accounts with a substantial amount of storage. In addition, both allowed files and folders to be shared, allowing her students to work in teams on the same document and share the same folders. She decided upon Google Drive because it also integrated Google Docs allowing her students to create their presentations using Google Slides.

She began by having students create a team project folder, which they shared with her and their teammates. Each team had to decide upon a unique team name, which is what they also named their project folder. Next, she had them create folders within their team's project folder; one for each type of media they would be collecting (i.e., documents, images, video, and audio). Finally, she had them create a slides file and save it in their project folder.

Before the students began their research, Mary discussed with the class the importance of choosing the right name for a file. She projected a picture of a San Francisco Cable Car and then asked what they thought they should name that file if they were to download and save it in the image folder for later use. By having them practice naming various items in this way, they began to get an idea of how to choose names that would help them remember what the item might be just from looking at the file name.

Next, Mary had them create a document for each type of information or data they were required to collect and gather (i.e., weather, food, maps, and transportation costs). These were named as such and placed in the documents folder. As students began to do their research on their vacation destination, they saved the various media they would need for their presentation into their respective folders. While they did so, Mary checked to see how the students were naming their files and if they were saving them in the correct folders, providing help when needed.

Because the presentation and media files were stored in Google Drive and shared between the team of students and Mary, all were able to see the work from anywhere provided they had Internet access and could log into their Google Account. This allowed Mary to project the completed presentations to the class so the team could then present it to their classmates.

By integrating and embedding the technology tools within the lesson, the multimedia presentation and other organizational materials gave her students the opportunity to demonstrate their products to assess the outcomes from the social studies and science standards. In addition, she was also teaching them how to best manage digital media with good file-naming and saving habits. This is an essential skill in today's digital world.

SUMMARY

In order to integrate technology in ways that will help students have a good understanding of basic concepts, it is important for teachers to have a good foundation as well. The primary objective of this chapter was to provide a solid foundation of basic technology concepts and operations. Basic computer information processing and storage operations were compared and contrasted to human brain functions to provide some frame of reference.

In addition, the chapter also discussed the need for classroom teachers to be familiar with and able to configure computers to take advantage of the equitable access tools for special needs students. These tools are readily available on all computers to help ease the access for all.

The scenario given in this chapter described how a teacher taught good data-saving habits using an online storage tool. Class projects that include a lot of digital files can become cumbersome without an understanding of proper file naming and file management. Regardless of the storage device chosen, these are skills that will serve both teachers and students alike.

REFERENCES AND RESOURCES

Apple. (2015). Accessibility. iOS. Retrieved from https://www.apple.com/accessibility/ios/.

Atkinson, R. C., and Shriffin, R. M. (1968). Human memory: A proposed system and its control processes. In R. W. Spence and J. T. Spence (eds.). *The psychology of learning and motivation* (vol. 2, pp. 89–195). New York: Academic.

Canonical Ltd. (2015). About Ubuntu. Retrieved from: http://www.ubuntu.com/about/about-ubuntu.

Computer Hope. (2016). *Basic computer troubleshooting.* Retrieved from: http://www.computerhope.com/basic.htm.

Dropbox. (2016). Dropbox. Retrieved from: https://www.dropbox.com/.

Free Software Foundation, Inc. (2015). Gimp—The GNU image manipulation program. Retrieved from: http://www.gimp.org/.

Google. (2015). Google Docs: Create and edit documents online, for free. Retrieved from: https://www.google.com/docs/about/.

Google. (2015). Google Drive: A safe place for all your files. Retrieved from: https://www.google.com/drive/.

Lasa Charity UK, Ltd. (2006). Lasa Knowledgebase. Retrieved from: http://ictknowledgebase.org.uk/linuxaccessibility.

Microsoft. (2016). Microsoft Accessibility. Retrieved from: https://www.microsoft.com/enable/.

Microsoft. (2016). OneDrive. Retrieved from: https://onedrive.live.com.

Mozilla. (2015a). Firefox web browser. Retrieved from: https://www.mozilla.org/en-US/firefox/new/.

Mozilla. (2015b). Mozilla Thunderbird. Retrieved from: https://www.mozilla.org/en-US/thunderbird/.

National Academies Press. (1996). *National Science Education Standards (NSES)*. Retrieved from: http://www.nap.edu/openbook.php?record_id=4962.

National Council for Social Studies. (2015). *National curriculum standards for social studies: A framework for teaching, learning and assessment*. Retrieved from: http://www.socialstudies.org/standards.

Open Source Initiative. (2015). Welcome to the open source initiative. Retrieved from: http://opensource.org/.

Reviews.com. LLC. (2016). *The best of everything: The 4 best cloud storage for students*. Retrieved from: http://www.reviews.com/cloud-storage/students/.

Sourceforge.net. (2015). Audacity: Free audio editor and recorder. Retrieved from: http://audacity.sourceforge.net/.

The Document Team. (2015). LibreOffice (Version 5.0.4) [Software]. Available from: http://www.documentfoundation.org/.

Chapter 5

Global Digital Citizenship

Given the interconnectivity of today's computer networks, students can gather information and resources, download just about any kind of media, and communicate with people around the world. It is the classroom teacher's responsibility to help his or her students understand the appropriate use of technologies and digital media. This chapter details various elements of digital citizenship and provides an example of teaching students what it means to be a good digital citizen, indeed a good global digital citizen.

GLOBAL INTERCONNECTION

Technology enables students to expand their learning environment beyond the confines of the classroom walls to connect with other learners globally. With smartphone applications they can communicate with people across the room or across the oceans. They have access to information, images, animations, audio, and video. Indeed, today's technology tools support students in many ways, from allowing them to develop and create media-rich digital reports and presentations to communicating and interacting with folks around the world.

As educators, we want students to have access to these powerful tools to enhance their learning opportunities, whether it is through access to vast information and resources or by communicating with people of other cultures. We want students to become part of and behave as good citizens of this global digital society, but with these opportunities come great responsibilities.

Inappropriate use of technology is a grave concern. To combat cyberbullying, most states in the United States now have laws and legislation to help solve this serious issue. Most schools and/or districts require students to sign an "appropriate use" policy, which outlines the dos and don'ts of using technology while at school. Many schools limit or restrict some technology use by students, for example, through a no-cell phone policy, which prohibits cell phone usage in school.

Szoka and Thiere (2009) believe that limiting access to technology, such as cell phones, limits learning opportunities and suggest that education is preferable to restrictive policies and legislation. They feel that instead of limiting a student's access to digital tools, educators should focus on teaching students to understand appropriate behavior and making good choices when they use technology.

Students will be using their cell phones and other technologies outside of school. Therefore, it is important to teach students appropriate and socially responsible technology use, both within and outside of school. In other words, students should be taught what it means to be good digital citizens within the digital society within which we all now belong.

DIGITAL CITIZENSHIP

Mike Ribble (2015) outlines nine themes of digital citizenship that should be considered with regard to three concepts: respect, education, and protection that should be taught right from kindergarten. The nine themes include: (1) digital access, (2) digital commerce, (3) digital communication, (4) digital literacy, (5) digital etiquette, (6) digital law, (7) digital rights and responsibilities, (8) digital health and wellness, and (9) digital security. One way of thinking about teaching these concepts is to group them into teachable elements.

Digital Literacy

Teaching students to be good digital citizens should start with digital literacy. Becoming literate and purposeful users of technology is one of the foundations that will serve them well. However, it is also important for students to know that because of the constant changes in technology, digital literacy doesn't end; they need to be lifelong learners.

Specifically, good digital citizens need to be aware that there are many new technologies becoming available continually and that one needs to keep honing and helping others hone their technology skills. However, digital literacy is not just about learning new technologies. Although these digital tools provide great opportunities, they also have inherent dangers.

Students need to become aware of the nature and responsibilities of free speech and being able to balance this double-edged sword when communicating electronically. For example, it could be easy to forget that there is a human being at the end of every communication and that appropriate etiquette should always be sought and taught when digitally interacting with others.

Social media tools can easily cause harm when students lack care in their communications. Traditional or cyberbullying can both be harmful for targeted children (Modecki et al., 2014). For students to become good digital citizens they must be taught the importance of being tolerant and compassionate when using electronic communication tools.

Students also need to become familiar with healthy habits of ergonomics for physical and intellectual well-being by learning about possible harm from the technological world we now live within. In particular, they should become aware of and keep up to date on security issues for personal identity and safety. It is vital for them to understand that their personal information should never be made readily available online. In addition to personal safety, students should also become familiar with and practice protecting ones data and equipment from viral attacks and electronic malfunctions by following good file backup practices.

Digital Commerce and Law

We live in a world of digital commerce where goods and services are bought and sold daily. While this aspect of today's life might seem normal to many, it hasn't been too many years since this trend first began. Because lawmaking is much slower than technology developments, some of the laws and regulations to govern digital commerce are still being written. Students need to become aware of issues that will impact their lives. For example, the electronic marketplace operates from many different nations. Foreign laws and regulations often vary and may be in conflict with those of which one may be aware.

Over the past decade, advances in technology have brought copyright issues to the forefront as many artists now distribute their works via the Internet. A good example is iTunes (Apple, 2015). Students need to understand, comply with, and teach others respect for and appropriate use of digital media, including music, art, and words. In addition, good digital citizens do no harm to the work of others, nor do they invade privacy. They need to understand that illegally downloading music, videos, or images is copyright infringement.

There are, however, times when what may look like a copyright infringement is really "fair use." In addition, there are some "works" that are not limited by copyright, which means that one can freely download and use these works—it is not considered to be piracy. There are many "open-source" or "general public licensed" software that is freely available to download and install. This can cause a bit of confusion and copyright laws can be tricky for some teachers. Luckily, there are many resources to help teachers and their students learn the specifics of such laws.

Ethics

Students are often required to research information and then write a report to demonstrate what they've learned. Certainly, search engines and the Internet make this task much easier and, in a sense, more powerful because of the vast amount of information and resources available at a student's finger tips. Because of the ease of copying and pasting text from a website to a document, it is easy to fall prey to plagiarism. Without a good understanding of the appropriate use of materials and resources and citing one's sources, many students have plagiarized the works of others.

For students to be ethical researchers and writers, it is vital for them to respect another's original work. Perhaps, one of the best resources to help students learn good citation habits is Purdue's Online Writing Lab (Purdue OWL, 2016), a website that outlines APA and MLA writing styles.

Copyright and Fair Use

Copyright laws protect authors' literary, dramatic, musical, artistic, and other creative works and prevents others profiting from original works. However, copyright laws vary between countries, and this is an important point to consider when thinking about being a global digital citizen. For example, although many countries have ratified the Berne Convention treaty that protects artistic works, other countries have not, some disregarding copyright protection altogether (World Intellectual Property Organization, 2015).

One of the best resources available that can provide some quick answers to questions regarding US Copyright issues is the Frequently Asked Questions (available at copyright.gov/help/faq/faq-general.html#protect). US Copyright begins to protect an original work "the moment it is created and fixed in a tangible form that it is perceptible either directly or with the aid of a machine or device" (para. 4). In other words, an author is not required to register their work with the US Copyright Office to be copyright protected, although it is recommended.

Therefore, if a student comes across an image they want to use, unless it states otherwise, it is copyrighted. If a student creates an original work, it could be copyright protected, but it depends upon the state as some states have regulations regarding minors doing business dealings that involve copyright.

It may seem that since every work of art is copyrighted the moment it is posted online, the best approach to helping students become good digital citizens is to not allow them to download any digital media. However, there is an element of Copyright Law that permits the use of copyrighted material without it being a copyright infringement. "fair use" limits exclusive rights for copyrighted material and original works so that they can be used without breaking the law.

According to the US Copyright Office (2015), the factors that determine "fair use" of original copyrighted material includes: "(a) the purpose and character of the use, including whether such use is of a commercial nature or is for nonprofit educational purposes; (b) the nature of the copyrighted work; (c) the amount and substantiality of the portion used in relation to the copyrighted work as a whole; and (d) the effect of the use upon the potential market for or value of the copyrighted work" (para. 107).

In other words, teachers and students can use copyrighted material if it falls under fair use. This means that for many classroom activities, depending upon the copyrighted material, and that provided the work (that includes copyrighted digital media) is not published, is not going to be sold, and doesn't include a substantial amount of the copyrighted whole, it will fall under the fair use policy.

Open-Source and General Public License

While most software and digital media is copyrighted there are many resources that are open to the public and freely available. The General Public License movement and Open Source Initiative are resources of which all classroom teachers should be fully aware. By teaching and modeling the use of these freely available resources teachers will be helping their students become more digitally literate and better able to resist the temptation of becoming software pirates by alleviating the need for the illegal acquisition of software.

The "Quick Guide to GPLv3" (Free Software Foundation, Inc., 2014) states: "Nobody should be restricted by the software they use. There are four freedoms that every user should have: (a) the freedom to use the software for any purpose, (b) the freedom to change the software to suit your needs, (c) the freedom to share the software with your friends and neighbors, and (d) the freedom to share the changes you make. When a program offers users all of these freedoms, we call it free software" (para. 2).

Open-source software includes OSs, productivity tools, and various other applications that can be downloaded for free. In addition, there are many other free software titles available for educators. A great resource is the open-source school management software programs for teachers and students (Opensource.com, 2015).

Digital Access

Good digital citizens need to be aware that not all have the same access to technology tools and resources and that equitable access is a goal to which he or she should be committed. There are social, economic, and political barriers that might limit digital access both in the United States and globally. Certainly, if a student doesn't have access to technology, whether it be computers or the Internet, their resources are limited. Additionally, if digital access is limited because of censorship, whether it is for safety or political reasons, it is then not equitable to those who do not have those limitations.

Other students may not have equitable access, but not due to the lack of computers at home and/or school or censorship but because they have special needs that limit their digital access, such as a physical, visual, hearing, or other impairment. Classroom teachers should be aware that any limiting factor to digital access is inequitable access. Helping students to become good digital citizens includes teaching them how they might help others access technology.

Teachers should become familiar with the equitable access tools that are built into all computer OSs to support various special needs users. There are several ways to change the configuration of the computer to enhance the access for a variety of impairments related to vision, hearing, physical and motor skills, as well as learning and literacy. In addition, there are software applications that can be installed to further support folks with special needs. For example, those with vision loss can purchase commercial screen readers for Windows-based computers, such as Job Access with Speech (Freedom Scientific, Inc., 2015).

Teaching students to be good digital citizens means that they should become aware of social inequities and how these constraints limit access, thus helping students understand and gain a broader perspective and expand their global awareness. Good digital citizens are aware that limitations to digital access can be economic or political in nature, but it can also be due to one's special needs, that is, the inability to see, hear, and manipulate technologies. Indeed, a good digital citizen is aware of and works toward the goal of equitable access, regardless of any limitations.

GLOBAL DIGITAL CITIZENSHIP

Crawford and Kirby (2008) describe how technology can support global education, which helps students see themselves as global citizens: "The infusion of global education in K12 schooling thought the appropriate and effective use of various technologies is essential. By incorporating numerous technologies in authentic and meaningful ways in social studies teaching and learning, as supported by the technological pedagogical content knowledge (TPCK) framework, teachers can foster students' understandings about the interrelationships of peoples worldwide, thereby preparing students to think as global citizens" (p. 71).

Picardo (2012) discusses the opportunities for character-building experiences in study abroad programs: "Global awareness and international collaboration during the formative years results in more rounded individuals, encouraging our pupils to see things from different perspectives and helping them to make informed decisions, acquiring transferable skills that will be useful to them and will remain with them for life" (para. 10).

Although not the same experience as a study abroad program, students can connect with others internationally by using technologies such as Twitter and Skype. Setting up international collaborations (e.g., through ePals, a global online learning community) can offer students the opportunity to interact with others of differing cultures. They may quickly discover that they have more or perhaps less access to technology resources and tools than their international peers. This type of activity may greatly enhance the opportunity for students to discuss and reflect upon the first theme of digital citizenship—digital access—especially if there is no equitable access for all.

This type of international collaboration may increase opportunities to discuss and reflect upon other digital citizenship themes, such as digital commerce, digital law, and digital security. The global experience of an international collaboration can provide a contextual foundation to discuss, reflect, and practice digital etiquette given the possible cross-cultural differences that may influence the interaction, perhaps positively, perhaps negatively.

With social media, electronic messaging, and Internet-based applications, students can communicate in a more global environment. Integrating technology on a global scale can help students gain a better understanding of other cultures as they become aware of cultural differences. Teaching students appropriate ways of communicating via the digital tools can help them gain a more global perspective of greater tolerance and cultural understanding. As students gain an expanded global awareness they also will learn about their digital rights and responsibilities as global digital citizens within this global community.

SCENARIO: PREPARING GLOBAL DIGITAL CITIZENS

Debra is a fifth-grade teacher in Ohio who wants to design a unit that will teach her students about digital citizenship. In addition to wanting them to gain an understanding of the digital citizenship elements, she also wants to add the global component. The main objective of this unit is digital citizenship, but she also wants to integrate language arts outcomes.

Debra uses ePals (2015) to connect with Sierra, a fifth-grade teacher in Mexico, and suggests that they each have their students create an e-book that discusses the specifics of their respective locations. Sierra likes the idea as her students are also learning English and because she wants to include a language component for them. Debra has been to Mexico and knows some Spanish and Sierra knows some English. Between the two they are able to communicate fairly well.

While discussing their ideas together, they outline the criteria that should be met. Specifically, they will have their students work in teams where each team will select a specific element of their home cities, which will be the topic of their e-book. The elements will include topics from a local perspective, that is, local holidays and celebrations, fashion, favorite foods, popular culture, hobbies, and school activities. Each team of students will need to agree upon items that fall into each category for their e-book.

The e-book will need to include a variety of digital media such as images, audio, and video. The text in each team's e-book should be in both Spanish and English. Students will also record themselves narrating their text, as this will help support Sierra's language objective. Debra also liked the idea and believes having her students learn some Spanish will help them better understand the nature of this cross-cultural experience.

They decide that while each team works on their e-book, each student will be responsible for one section. This will provide for individual accountability and individual summative assessment. All media and other resources used in the e-books must be referenced and follow copyright laws according to their home countries.

To help support the project Debra and Sierra each created a Dropbox (2015) for their students' media files. Debra also created a project website using Google Sites (Google, 2015a) where the teams could share their e-books, which also provides the option for students to view and then post constructive comments regarding their counterparts' e-books. The project website would also house a repository of lesson plans and other resources that the teachers may want to share. Debra plans to have her students use iBook Author, the e-book authoring tool that is available in her school's Macintosh computers that can save files in iBook and PDF format.

Debra and Sierra decide that each will write up their lesson plans and post them on the project website so one can see how the other will proceed. By doing so, they can share activities, mini lessons, and assessment ideas. There will also be a variety of resources linked to Google Sites, such as the locations of copyright-free images, audios, and videos. A link to Google Translate

(Google, 2015b) will provide a resource for both teachers and students to help them translate student texts from English to Spanish and from Spanish to English.

Debra and Sierra discuss the technology needs for the project over Skype (2015). While Debra's students will be able to create their e-books using Macintosh computers with iBook Author, Sierra's students will not. However, Sierra does have a class set of six iPads (Apple, 2015) and computers in the school lab with wireless Internet access. After a brief search they also find Creative Book Builder (Ng, 2015), which Sierra's students can use to create their e-books. It is relatively inexpensive, but yet powerful and easy to learn. It should serve well for the project.

As they move forward, they decide to save the e-books in some compatible format, like PDF, to make it easier for each class to view the others' e-books. In addition to having the students use their cell phones and the school's digital cameras to take pictures, they can also use Internet media to help fulfill some of the digital media requirements. Both the Macintosh and iPads (Apple, 2015) can also record audio, which will support the students narrating their text.

Although Debra and Sierra will be sharing their lesson and assessment plans, each works independently as each has specific objectives, outcomes, and learning expectations for their respective students. So, Debra begins to design her lesson plans by first identifying her specific unit objectives and then deciding upon an assessment strategy.

Wanting her students to become good digital citizens, she believes that her objectives for this unit should include all nine themes of Ribble's (2015) definition. However, she decides that while some might be taught implicitly though a series of mini lessons, others might discussed after further reflection on this cross cultural experience. For example, she believes that her first mini lessons should be on digital health and wellness, security, and law.

She also plans a mini lesson on digital communication and etiquette, as this will be important when students begin to interact with their Mexican peers. She also wants to have a class discussion about digital access, commerce, and rights and responsibilities. For example, there may be a situation or issue that comes up due to cross-cultural differences during the project, which could easily turn into a teachable moment. These elements can be discussed when the project is over during a "how-did-it-go" debriefing with the students.

Engaging in a project of creating e-books can also be a great vehicle for teaching and assessing language arts outcomes. Debra believes the unit will help her students demonstrate their meeting the Common Core English Language Arts Writing Standards for fifth-grade students that state that students should be able to:

- Conduct short research projects that use several sources to build knowledge through investigation of different aspects of a topic.
- Recall relevant information from experiences or gather relevant information from print and digital sources; summarize or paraphrase information in notes and finished work, and provide a list of sources. (p. 21)

Each team will be required to create a concept map and then turn it into an outline of their e-book. She plans on using this as a formative assessment for each team's progress, in terms of the criteria for cultural content and organization. She also plans on meeting with each team during the development process to observe students' writing and media collections. This observation also serves as a formative assessment of their individual and group progress.

Each team is required to create a spreadsheet or other document where each student will log the location from where each media file was acquired. During her team meetings she also will review the log to assess each student's media acquisition. The log will also include a references section where all citations for media, links, and other resources are listed. Both of these will serve as her summative assessment for the outcome of digital law and the Common Core #8 outcome of "providing a list of sources."

Debra will be using the team's final e-book as the summative assessment item for the Common Core outcomes. In addition, it will also help her assess her students' achievement of the digital citizenship theme, digital literacy. In other words, she will be able to gage how well each student did in creating their page within their team's e-book. However, she will also need to assess the other eight digital citizenship themes. Debra will use the comments students made on their peers' e-books within the project website section and also review any email communications to assess her students' engagement using etiquette through their digital communication.

After the "how-did-it-go" debriefing Debra plans on having each student respond to items in their reflection journals. In it, each will be asked to reflect upon the experience and address all of the following questions or statements: (1) How did you work in a healthy manner? (2) List at least three things that you did to keep your personal information and data safe. (3) What did you learn about copyright while creating and sharing your e-book with students from another country? (4) Do you think that everyone had equitable access to digital resources? (5) What does it mean to have digital rights and responsibilities?

SUMMARY

Given this global society, where students have instant access to information, media, and individuals around the world, it is vital that they learn what it means to be a good global digital citizen. Classroom teachers are expected to help their students understand the appropriate use of technology in all phases of learning. Students should be aware of and practice safe and secure technology use. Digital literacy includes an awareness of digital commerce, obeying digital laws, and practicing appropriate use of technology for communication, publishing, and productivity—understanding their digital rights and responsibilities.

The scenario for this chapter provided an example of international collaboration, which to be successful takes a lot of planning and coordination between teachers. Often it's necessary for each teacher to be able to assess different academic objectives and there needs to be flexibility in terms of access to technology. However, this type of a cross-cultural collaboration could also result in possible miscommunication. While that is the nature of learning from cross-cultural interactions, teachers engaged in this type of collaboration need to be flexible but yet provide rules, regulations, and agreements on how best to handle any miscommunication issues.

However, miscommunications provide teachable moments for students to gain greater global awareness and to better their understanding of cultural differences. As they do so, students will also enhance their understanding of their rights and responsibilities and the tenets and behaviors of global digital citizenship within the global digital society.

REFERENCES AND RESOURCES

Apple. (2015). Apple. Retrieved from: https://www.apple.com.
Copyright Law Office. (2015). Copyright Law: Chapter 1. Retrieved from: http://www.copyright.gov/title17/92chap1.html#107.
Crawford, E. O., and Kirby, M. M. (2008). Fostering students' global awareness: Technology applications in social studies teaching and learning. *Journal of Curriculum and Instruction, 2* (1), 56–73.
Dropbox. (2015). Dropbox. Retrieved from: https://www.dropbox.com/.
ePals. (2015). *Where learners connect.* Retrieved from: http://www.epals.com/.
Free Software Foundation, Inc. (2014). A Quick Guide to GPLv3—GNU Project. Retrieved from: http://www.gnu.org/licenses/quick-guide-gplv3.html.
Freedom Scientific, Inc. (2015). JAWS Screen Reader—Best in Class. Retrieved from: http://www.freedomscientific.com/Products/Blindness/JAWS.
Google. (2015a). Google Sites. Retrieved from: https://sites.google.com/.
Google. (2015b). Google Translate. Retrieved from: https://translate.google.com/.
Modecki, K. L., Minchin, J., Harbaugh, A. G., Guerra, N. G., and Runions, K. C. (2014). Bullying prevalence across contexts: A meta-analysis measuring cyber and traditional bullying. *Journal of Adolescent Health, 55* (5), 602–11.
Ng, T. (2015). Creative Book Builder v3.2 (CBB). Retrieved from: http://getcreative-bookbuilder.blogspot.com/2015/05/creative-book-builder-v32.html.

Opensource.com. (2015). A review of open source software programs for school management. Reviewed from: http://opensource.com/life/13/1/three-open-source-school-management-software-programs-teachers-and-student.

Open Source Initiative. (2015). Welcome to the open source initiative. Retrieved from: http://opensource.org/.

Picardo, J. (2012). *Why students need global awareness and understandings of other cultures.* Retrieved from: http://www.theguardian.com/teachernetwork/2012/sep/25/studentsglobalawarenessothercultures.

Ribble, M. (2015). *Nine elements.* Retrieved from: http://www.digitalcitizenship.net/Nine_Elements.html.

Skype. (2015). Skype. Retrieved from: http://www.skype.com.

Szoka, B. M., and Thierer, A. D. (2009). Cyberbullying legislation: Why education is preferable to regulation. *Progress & Freedom Foundation Progress on Point Paper, 16* (12).

The Purdue Online Writing Lab. (Purdue OWL). (2016). Retrieved from: https://owl.english.purdue.edu/.

World Intellectual Property Organization. (2015). Berne Convention for the Protection of Literary and Artistic Works. Retrieved from: http://www.wipo.int/treaties/en/ip/berne/.

Chapter 6

Communication and Collaboration

With today's digital communication tools, it is possible for students to work collaboratively, thus expanding their ability to support and enhance their learning and contribute to the learning of others. This chapter will discuss specific digital communication and collaboration tools that support student learning in a variety of way. By learning how to use these tools, students have an opportunity to gain a better understanding of how to collaborate with peers, experts, and others to share ideas, contribute to team projects, create shared original works, and solve problems.

DIGITAL COMMUNICATION AND COLLABORATION TOOLS

With only an Internet connection and a browser, students have been able to engage with others across vast distances using a variety of communication tools, such as email, discussion boards, chat rooms, and instant messaging. While these text-based tools have provided opportunities for students to communicate, interact, and even collaborate, there are new digital communication and collaboration tools being developed every day.

Audio-video conferencing tools allow students not only to communicate but also to edit the same document at the same time. Crenzel and Nojima in 2006 quote Claire, who was eight years old at the time, explaining why she prefers interactive communication: "The TV is just there, and you just sit and watch and do nothing. I just can't stand to do nothing. Messenger is a lot better: you talk and someone talks back to you, it's a lot more fun" (p. 6). Now, a decade later, consider what Claire at eighteen years of age might think about today's free video conferencing tools such as Skype (2015) or Google Hangouts (2015).

It is important to remember, however, that students have greater responsibilities when using these powerful communication tools and they need to understand and practice good global digital citizenship. It is important for students to use etiquette when interacting with others regardless of where they may be located. Digital safety and security must also be considered by both teachers and parents. There are tools that can help secure these interactive environments, such as classroom-safe applications and websites of which one should become aware. In addition to providing great teacher resources, Common Sense Education (Common Sense Media Inc., 2016) provides online tools that helps students achieve a Digital Passport (https://www.commonsensemedia.org/educators/digital-passport).

Digital communication tools, particularly the use of mobile phones, have changed the way we communicate (Henley, 2010). Indeed, they are used for just about every kind of communication (voice, textual, and visual) and even changed the way we communicate. For example, we now might not call a friend and have a long conversation about going out for dinner. Rather, after a brief exchange of texts, without ever talking with them, we can communicate our intentions and agree on plans.

Given the different ways some of these tools are used, many fall into the category of *social media* and are designed to allow people to share and exchange elements of their lives through comments, ideas, photos, and videos. Think about how differently one communicates using text, Twitter (2015), Instagram (2015), email, discussion boards, and/or a forum.

Synchronous and Asynchronous Tools

Today's digital tools have changed how we communicate and have caused educators and researchers to rethink the notion of literacy and teaching (Walsh, 2008; Sweeny, 2010; Bogard and McMackin, 2012). A few asynchronous communication tools provide some element of time for reflective writing, while others are synchronous—happening at the same time. Even though texting is asynchronous, think about how fast one receives and replies to a message. Because communicating via text can be so swift and many digital devices have limited keyboards for typing, users often utilize abbreviations (e.g., LOL, BFF, IMHO, BTW, etc.).

Using synchronous tools for a class or group discussion requires that users interact in real time. Having to reply very quickly requires students to respond with their immediate thoughts. However, because they are immediate, there may be little to no reflection. Also, a student's keyboarding skills may impact his or her ability to engage in a swiftly moving discussion, thus leaving him or her out of the conversation.

Texting and/or SMS Clicker Student Response Systems can also be used for instant assessment of student understanding. While not synchronous, teachers can check very quickly for their students' general understandings of concepts. Teachers can also take instant polls by having students use clickers to respond to questions, which then are immediately displayed as a pie chart representing the graphical breakdown of the class' opinion on a topic. While these can be powerful tools, Student Response Systems can be expensive.

Email is used by many classroom teachers to communicate with students and their parents in various ways by sending out announcements, newsletters, or individual communiques. Teachers can also have their students use email as a way to learn good writing skills by having them practice formal writing. Rather than allowing students to sloppily write down their thoughts or ideas in an email, a teacher can have their students collect their thoughts, compose their ideas, and refine their writing in a word processor to practice good sentence structure, grammar, spelling, and punctuation.

Blogs (web logs) allow students to journal and publish their thoughts or comments in a personal online space. Blogs can be configured to be private, available to only those invited, or visible to the world. Having students create their own blogs gives them opportunities to share their thoughts or understandings of or reflections upon a topic. In one example, Lacina and Griffith (2012) describe fourth-grade students using their blogs to support reading instruction, specifically the reading strategy of prediction. After the teacher reads the first half of a book she then asks her students to write their predictions of what will happen next.

Wikis are tools that provides for online communication and collaboration, Wikipedia (2015) being the most famous wiki. In addition to open-source wiki applications that can be set up on a school server for teachers and students, Google Sites (2015) permits users to set up free, private, shared, or open-to-the-public websites where students can coauthor web pages, have discussions, and post files. By coauthoring a publication in this manner, students contribute to their group's or team's effort to produce an original work.

Learning Management Systems

Blackboard (2015) or the open-source Moodle (2015) are good examples of learning management systems (LMS). These tools provide an online learning area for content, as well as a variety of digital communication and collaboration tools in a private and safe learning environment. They also include elements to provide for a host of other tools, such as information presentations, grade books, assignment drop boxes, and learner tracking.

While many school districts provide an LMS to support pre-K–12 classroom teachers, there are other tools that teachers can access for free. Edmodo (2015) is a similar application for all grade levels. Once teachers create an Edmodo account, they can create a class environment where they can post assignments, resources, and practice items. One of the powerful elements of an Edmodo account is that it can also embed lesson plans, which are directly aligned to specific Common Core Standards, for both English language arts and mathematics.

Social Media Tools

Twitter, a very popular social media tool, allows users to post messages that include a maximum of 140 characters and up to four images in one *tweet*. Because of the limited characters for a message, Twitter could be considered a microblogging tool used as a way to share, present, or announce information. Teachers might have their students follow their Twitter accounts to provide announcements. Borau et al. (2009) describes how teachers have their students use Twitter to practice and enhance their English language skills.

Instagram, another social media tool, allows users to share elements of their lives through photographs, which can also be linked to provide direct feeds to their Facebook account. Blair and Serafini (2014) describe integrating a variety of social media tools into the classroom, suggesting that teachers have their students create a video book review and then posting it to their Instagram account. English language learners can practice language skills by creating full-text photo-essays on specific topics or themes, such as illustrating science or other academic projects.

Facebook is probably the best-known social media tool, but integrating it into a classroom requires some forethought and care. Teachers commenting on their students' posts and spreading their personal beliefs and stories have impacted student motivation and affected learning and classroom climate because students felt that it was a bit of an invasion into their out-of-school lives (Mazer et al., 2007; Munoz and Towner, 2009). However, Hull (2014) described how a high-school teacher created a class Facebook page, which was more about the class than the teacher, and helped create a sense of community and keep high-school students informed on relevant events and activities.

WEB 2.0 FOR LEARNING: LEARNER-GENERATED CONTENT

Web 2.0 websites are sites where the users generate the content. For example, the Meredith Corporation's Recipe.com (2015) is a Web 2.0 website, which might be better termed a *web service* because users create accounts and then post their recipes to share with others. Facebook is probably the most well known of all Web 2.0 websites as all of the users create the content with their profile and posts.

Web 2.0 Classroom Examples

There are many Web 2.0 website resources for both elementary and secondary classroom teachers. One good example of a safe and free resource is Storybird (2015) a website where students can collaborate to write, illustrate, and publish stories and books in a shared but safe environment. Students can access Storybird through computers or tablets. Teacher accounts support creating a protected area to manage students and post assignments.

Another very popular example is Glogster (2015). Students access the website using computers or tablets and create *glogs*, or electronic posters, on teacher-assigned topics using predesigned graphics or images from the Internet. Teachers can create a class account, which provides a safe location for their class to create and share their glogs.

Collaborative Productivity Tools

Online productivity tools are designed to support collaboration where students can work at the same time on a shared document. Google Docs (Google, 2015b) permit sharing, thus allowing collaboration and coauthoring. Microsoft OneDrive Live (2015) also provides free use of the online suite of productivity tools, which allows for sharing and coediting of documents, spreadsheets, slide shows, and other files. Using these tools permits coauthoring by students who are located anywhere around the globe provided they have Internet access. This provides a good opportunity for students to work with others regardless of their location.

USING DIGITAL COMMUNICATION AND COLLABORATION TOOLS SAFELY

While Google is a great search engine, it can find and display information, images, and other media that are simply not for children. This is an important factor that all school districts must bear in mind. A few have gone to the extent of censoring some websites or specific content, which limits how an open network functions.

KidzSearch.com (2015) and KidRex (2015) are kid-safe search engines powered by Google that filters content to provide kid-safe information. Wikipedia for Kids (2015) also provides safe information and is available on mobile devices, that is, through Wiki for Kids (2015). There are also many international organizations available to help teachers make connections with other teachers for collaborations. Kid World Citizen (2015) helps teachers connect their students to other students globally.

In addition to being able to use a search engine to access just about any kind of content, students can also connect with others using a variety of powerful communication and collaboration tools that are not limited to the usual text-based communication and collaboration systems. They can also use Internet conferencing systems, such as Skype® and Elluminate® that provide synchronous audio-video communication. All they need for this is an inexpensive headset and microphone.

Although Skypito® (2008) is designed in cooperation with Skype and provides a safe online communication tool for children between the ages of two and fourteen, a confined learning management system could be considered safer because all of the communication and collaboration happens within the enclosed system. However, when students create their personal learning environment using Web 2.0 and other open communication and collaboration tools, it provides greater opportunities for learning as they assemble, organize, and interact with others.

While permitting students to use more open communication and collaboration tools might provide greater opportunities for them to interact and learn on a more global scale, it brings up the safety issue. Some schools or districts require teachers to use specific tools or learning systems, such as Blackboard. Others may have few or no restrictions on how students use some of the tools discussed. Another option that many school districts are choosing is subscribing to the Google Classroom (Google, 2016), which includes Google Docs, Gmail, and Google Calendar in a free, safe, and secure web-based environment.

SCENARIO: WEB 2.0—BIRDS OF A FEATHER

Jenn, a fifth-grade teacher, has good Internet connectivity in her school and new computers in both her room and the school computer lab. She wants to design a unit where her students can communicate and collaborate using technology tools with other fifth graders. Jenn, who lives and teaches in the western part of the United States, plans to collaborate with her old college roommate Peggy, who teaches a similar grade level in the eastern part of the United States.

Jenn and Peggy decide on a unit where their students will use communication and collaboration tools to help them achieve the Next Generation Science Standards "Dimension 1: Scientific and Engineering Practices" where students are engaged in the process of real-life inquiry and data collection. Specifically, they want their students to demonstrate their understandings of NGSS: "LS2.A: Interdependent Relationships in Ecosystems." They also want them to achieve some of the Common Core Language Arts Standards of reading and writing within the context of science, which have been adopted by both of their states.

After a quick search, Jenn found a great Web 2.0 site that she believes Peggy and she can use for this unit and future units to help their students achieve the outcomes of these standards. The Cornell Lab of Ornithology (2015) provides great teacher resources, which include lesson plans, links to classroom kits, and information on how to integrate learning materials into science instruction. They even have nest webcams that broadcast nesting birds in real time.

The BirdSleuth mission states that "BirdSleuth K–12 creates innovative resources that build science skills while inspiring young people to connect to local habitats, explore biodiversity, and engage in citizen science projects" (para. 5).

Jenn and Peggy organize the unit using Google Hangouts and decide that their students will learn how to observe and record local bird sightings into an online bird observation database. The National Audubon Society and the Cornell Lab of Ornithology collaborated to develop the eBird (2015) website, which is an online database for recording bird observations to help indicate presence or absence of specific species within specific locations.

Anyone can create a free account to record their observations into the database in real time, which can also be used to search for information and data on specific bird species within specific locations. In other words, by integrating the eBird database into their unit, both Jenn's and Peggy's students can engage in real data collection based upon their actual observations that will then be shared with others around the world.

As the "Using eBird with Students Teacher's Guide" (Cornell Lab of Ornithology, 2015) states, "Explain to students that the data they collect is important to scientists. In order to provide complete and correct data, students need to be able to accurately identify and count birds. The data they collect will be used by professional scientists who need precise and accurate information in order to understand bird abundance and distribution" (para. 3).

Jenn and Peggy plan on using the vast resources on the BirdSleuth K–12 website to help teach their students how to identify and record bird species. Once each class has a good foundation of the process, Jenn and Peggy plan on taking their students on an initial bird observation field trip in each of their respective cities. This will help scaffold the observation and reporting process so that the students can later go on independent field trips for possible future lessons.

Students will record their observations using the bird count tally sheet provided by the BirdSleuth K–12 website and then summarize them into one master checklist for each class. The classes will then plan a Google Hangouts session where they will compare and contrast their findings. In addition, students will be grouped into teams of three from each class (totaling six) to write up a collaborative report, which will detail the process, findings, and conclusions regarding the observed ecosystems.

Each team of six will create a Google Slides presentation, which will include graphs, images, and video and/or audio recordings that outline the planning, process, findings, analysis, and conclusions of their comparison of observations between the two classes. Each team will then present their reports to both classes using Google Hangouts.

Each student will select one bird from those observed by their team (either from their class or the other class) and use BirdSleuth K–12 and other resources to research information to gather specific details regarding their chosen bird, including habitat, food sources, life span, predators, and their analysis of that bird's ecosystem. Students will use Blogger (Google, 2015a) to create their individual bird report and write a blogpost that outlines their experience being a citizen scientist, which can be used for individual summative assessment.

SUMMARY

The purpose of this chapter was to provide readers with a solid foundation of digital communication and collaboration tools that can be integrated into classroom instruction in ways that are safe and powerful. Beginning with an overview of synchronous and asynchronous communication tools, the discussion moved to more complex synchronous video conferencing, Web 2.0 tools, and digital collaboration tools where learners can create content the same way they create digital artifacts to demonstrate their learning.

While integrating these digital communication: and collaboration tools can be powerful methods to enhance student learning, it is also very important that teachers have a good understanding of safety measures. Although communicating and collaborating with other learners and experts can provide more real-life learning experiences, there can also be dangers, as students will be in direct contact with others outside of their classroom, state, or even country.

While integrating digital tools such as today's social media—which is used by nearly everyone—might be exciting and cool, it must be done with care. Teachers need to remember that practicing good digital citizenship will set a good example to their students about the appropriate use of these powerful tools.

REFERENCES AND RESOURCES

BlackBoard, Inc. (2015). Retrieved from: http://www.blackboard.com/.

Blair, R., and Serafini, T. M. (2014). Integration of Education: Using Social Media Networks to Engage Students. *Systemics, Cybernetics and Informatics, 12* (6), 23–31.

Bogard, J. M., and McMackin, M. C. (2012). Combining traditional and new literacies in a 21st-century writing workshop. *The Reading Teacher, 65* (5), 313–23.

Borau, K., Ullrich, C., Feng, J., and Shen, R. (2009). Microblogging for language learning: Using twitter to train communicative and cultural competence. In *Advances in Web Based Learning–ICWL 2009* (pp. 78–87). Springer Berlin Heidelberg.

Common Core: State Standards Initiative. (2015). *English and Language Arts Standards.* Retrieved from: http://www.corestandards.org/ELA-Literacy/.

Common Sense Media Inc. (2016). Retrieved from: https://www.commonsensemedia.org/educators/digital-passport.

Cornell Lab of Ornithology. (2015). BirdSleuth K–12: Teachers. Retrieved from: http://www.birdsleuth.org/info-for-teachers/.

Cornell Lab of Ornithology. (2015). BirdSleuth K–12: Using eBirds with Students. Retrieved from: http://www.birdsleuth.org/using-ebird-with-students/.

Crenzel, S. R., and Nojima, V. L. (2006). Children and Instant Messaging. *Ergonomics 4 Children.*

Edmodo. (2015). Edmodo.Com: Connect with students and parents in your paperless classroom. Retrieved from: https://www.edmodo.com/.

Glogster EDU. (2015). Create and Explore Educational Content Online. Retrieved from: http://edu.glogster.com.

Google. (2015a). Blogger. Retrieved from: https://www.blogger.com/.

Google. (2015b). Google Docs. Retrieved from: https://www.google.com/docs/about/.

Google. (2015c). Google Hangouts. Retrieved from: https://plus.google.com/hangouts.

Google. (2016). *Google Classroom Help.* Retrieved from: https://support.google.com/edu/classroom/answer/6020279?hl=en.

Henley, J. (2010). Teenagers and technology: "I'd rather give up my kidney than my phone." *The Guardian.* Retrieved from: http://www.appohigh.org/ourpages/auto/2013/4/19/54668350/Teenagers%20and%20technology.docx.

Hull, K. (2014). Using Facebook in the classroom. *International Journal of Social Media and Interactive Learning Environments, 2* (1), 60–69.

Instagram.com. (2015). Retrieved from: https://instagram.com/.

KidRex.org. (2015). Safe Search for Kids, by Kids! Retrieved from: http://www.kidrex.org/.

Kid World Citizen. (2011). Get an International Pen-Pal. Retrieved from: http://kidworldcitizen.org/2011/11/11/pen-pal-programs/.

Kidzsearch.com. (2015). Kids Safe Search Engine Powered by Google. Retrieved from: http://www.kidzsearch.com/.

Lacina, J., and Griffith, R. (2012). Blogging as a means of crafting writing. *The Reading Teacher, 66* (4), 316–20.

Mazer, J. P., Murphy, R. E., and Simonds, C. J. (2007). I'll see you on "Facebook": The effects of computer-mediated teacher self-disclosure on student motivation, affective learning, and classroom climate. *Communication Education, 56* (1), 1–17.

Meredith Corporation. (2015). Recipe.com: Quick Recipes, Easy Meal Ideas. Retrieved from: http://recipe.com.

Microsoft OneDrive Live. (2015). Word, Excel, and PowerPoint on the Web. Retrieved from: https://office.live.com/start/default.aspx.

Moodle. (2015). Open-source learning platform. Retrieved from: https://moodle.org/.

Munoz, C., and Towner, T. (2009, March). Opening Facebook: How to use Facebook in the college classroom. In *Society for Information Technology & Teacher Education International Conference* (vol. 2009, no. 1, pp. 2623–27).

National Academy of Sciences. (2015). A Framework for K–12 Science Education: Practices, Crosscutting Concepts, and Core Ideas. Retrieved from: http://www.nap.edu/catalog.php?record_id=13165.

Skype.com. (2015). Free Calls to Friends and Family. Retrieved from: http://www.skype.com/en/.

Skypito.com. (2015). Retrieved from: http://www.skypito.com/.

Storybird Studio. (2015). Literacy and writing tools for teachers, librarians, educators and classrooms. Retrieved from: http://storybird.com/educators/.

Sweeny, S. M. (2010). Writing for the instant messaging and text messaging generation: Using new literacies to support writing instruction. *Journal of Adolescent & Adult Literacy, 54* (2), 121–30.

Twitter. (2015). Retrieved from: https://twitter.com/.

Walsh, M. (2008). Worlds have collided and modes have merged: Classroom evidence of changed literacy practices. *Literacy, 42* (2), 101–8.

Wiki for Kids. (2015). Wiki for Kids – Mobile Version. Retrieved from: http://www.wikiforkids.ws/.

Wikipedia for Kids. (2015). Safe Search for Kids. Retrieved from: http://www.safesearchkids.com/.

Wikipedia.org. (2015). Retrieved from: https://www.wikipedia.org/.

Chapter 7

Research, Data Collection, and Analysis

Although the Internet can be used in many ways to help students research and gather information, teachers need to help their students be information literate. While this is one way for students to conduct research, there are many other types of research that can be supported by digital tools that go beyond using the Internet as an electronic encyclopedia. Digital tools can be used to help students gather and analyze data, which can then be used to draw inferential conclusions on original research questions.

This chapter provides an overview or foundation for using digital tools to support student research and will discuss ways in which teachers can integrate these tools to support their students conducting original research, which includes information literacy, being able to define basic research questions, gathering and analyzing data, as well as drawing inferential conclusions on their findings.

RESEARCH, DATA COLLECTION, AND ANALYSIS

Using a web browser to gather information on the Internet can be powerful research tool. The Common Core English Language Arts Standards indicate that research and media are vital skills and themes for every grade level. "To be ready for college, workforce training, and life in a technological society, students need the ability to gather, comprehend, evaluate, synthesize, and report on information and ideas, to conduct original research in order to answer questions or solve problems, and to analyze and create a high volume and extensive range of print and non-print texts in media forms old and new" (p. 4).

However, it is vital that students can discriminate between good information and bad information, as it is very easy to publish anything on the Internet and make it globally available. Students need to be able to locate credible informational sources and create something with that information, for example, organize and share it in a report, use it to make informed decisions, and/or build new understandings that will then generate new questions to be investigated. Students must learn how to plan strategies that guide inquiry so they can locate, organize, analyze, evaluate, synthesize, and ethically use information.

GATHERING AND EVALUATING SOURCES

Students can easily run a Google Search (2015a) and find a great deal of information about their topic. Unfortunately, however, not all of the information is accurate or credible. In addition, because it is so easy for students to simply copy and paste the information they locate, they can plagiarize by passing it off as their own writing. Therefore, it is very important to ensure that students understand what it means to be a good digital citizen and a good consumer of information in terms of responsible use of digital resources.

While the Internet is the primary resource that students use today, it is important to help them understand that there are other informational resources such as traditional print media. Although rapidly changing to digital delivery, newspapers, magazines, and books can still be good sources for information that can broaden the student's research. Depending upon the level of their students, teachers may also want to consider the use of peer-reviewed journal articles. These can be especially rich in terms of providing reviews of research projects.

Soon after the World Wide Web became widely available, it became clear that students needed to be able to evaluate research sources, especially Internet sources and be aware about where they find information and who was responsible for creating it. Harris (2013) described Internet resources as being "on a continuum of reliability and quality" (p. 1), and provided the "CARS" checklist, which is a great resource for website evaluation in terms of *Credibility, Accuracy, Reasonableness, and Support.*

In addition to the CARS model, there are online tutorials to help students understand how to evaluate Internet findings. One such tutorial is Houghton Mifflin's *Using the Web: Finding and Evaluating Web Sites* (2015). While these tools will help students become good consumers of information found on the Internet, finding and appropriately citing credible information from the Internet is just the beginning of research.

ORIGINAL RESEARCH

In addition to the vast amounts of information available from various Internet sources, students also need to be able to use digital tools to conduct original research by collecting data to help them answer questions and solve problems. Teaching students to conduct original research supports the notion of Lewis and Smith's (1993) definition of higher order thinking: "when a person takes new information and information stored in memory and interrelates and/or rearranges and extends this information to achieve a purpose or find possible answers in perplexing situations" (p. 136).

Conducting original research provides students with skills that will help them use digital tools to solve complex issues and problems. However, teaching these skills requires teachers to be a bit more creative in developing lessons and units that engage their students in the research process. Conducting original research can be challenging and quite complex and it is important to adjust the research complexity to the age and abilities of the students. However, with appropriate research questions, support, and scaffolds, original research can be conducted by students of any age.

RESEARCH AND DATA TYPES

Original research always begins with posing a research question. The type of research question determines the type of data one must collect to help answer that question. Research is about answering questions with data; sometimes it is information indirectly reported from others, such as information gathered from the Internet. At other times, research questions must be answered by collecting original or raw data from the *field*. Collecting this kind of data from the original source supports real-life research by giving students responses to surveys and audio and/or video media files that once collected, reviewed, and analyzed will help answer the students research questions. However, it's important to understand that the research question will drive the research approach and subsequent data collection.

Quantitative Data

Data can be quantitative in nature like the numerical results from a basic survey. Let's say, for example, that a teacher wants her sixth graders to achieve Common Core Math 6-SP, Statistics and Probability (2015). A real-life research project might be to have students figure out what percentage of each ice cream flavor should be purchased for the sixth-grade end-of-the-year track-and-field day. The research question might be: "What are the most popular flavors of ice cream for all sixth graders in our school?"

To answer this question, students will ask their peers how many like vanilla, chocolate, strawberry flavors, etc. The easiest way to gather this information would be to have students create a survey using Google Forms (2015c), which would gather responses from the sixth graders to help answer this research question by filling in a radio button associated with vanilla, chocolate, strawberry, etc. As the surveys are submitted, Google Forms creates a spreadsheet that calculates all of the data inputted, proving a percentage for each flavor.

By completing the survey, students are providing numerical data to find out what percentage of them like each flavor of ice cream. While this is very basic, notice that the question is really asking *how many?*, which is a quantifiable element, that is, a number. Once the data is collected it can be analyzed in terms of statistics, that is mean, median, and mode, thus helping students achieve CC Math 6-SP by figuring out what percentage of ice cream should be purchased for each flavor.

Qualitative Data

Data can also be qualitative in nature, meaning that it might be someone's response to an open-ended question or audio or video from an observation or interview. Let's say that a teacher wants his sixth graders to achieve outcomes listed in Common Core English Language Arts writing standards for Literacy in History/Social Studies, specifically the outcome for "Research to Build and Present Knowledge # 7. Conduct short research projects to answer a question (including a self-generated question), drawing on several sources and generating additional related, focused questions that allow for multiple avenues of exploration" (2015, p. 66).

The research question might be: "What was it like to live in the Vietnam War years?" To answer this question, students would have to collect very different types of data. In this case, qualitative data that might include audio or video interviews with grandparents, old pictures taken at the time, maps of Vietnam, etc.

Students might collect old pictures, newspaper or magazine articles from the time, news video archives, and audio and video recorded interviews with folks who lived during that time that would then help them *interpret* what it might have been like to live during the Vietnam War era. Reviewing and analyzing this data would most likely generate more questions, which could lead down other avenues of exploration, thus demonstrating that they are meeting the outcome for "Research to Build and Present Knowledge # 7."

Qualitative data is not generally quantifiable in nature. Rather, this data helps students *interpret* answers to their research questions. Qualitative data is often collected by social scientists and educators to help them describe or provide accounts of events or phenomena in such a way as to help them draw inferences or interpretations. The reported findings, which can take many forms, are the researcher's *description* supported by the qualitative data that brings meaning and context to the event or phenomenon.

DIGITAL DATA COLLECTION TOOLS

It is important to understand that research questions often require mixed methods, meaning that both quantitative and qualitative data may need to be collected to provide the broadest description or overview of the research topic. There are a variety of digital tools that students can use to collect both types of data, which can then be organized and analyzed to help answer the research questions.

Scientific Sensing Probes

Several companies support science education by providing scientific data collection devices, software, and educator resources. Vernier Software and Technology (2015) offers many different wired and wireless sensing probes that students can use to gather data (i.e., to sense light, temperature, motion, UV rays, gases, heart rate, and a variety of other things) and send directly to iPads, smartphones, or laptops. They also provide curricula and even free software for science education from elementary through higher education.

Pasco Scientific (2015) is another company that offers scientific data collection devices, software, and educator resources. In addition to a variety of curricula for physics, biology, chemistry, earth, environmental, and general science for high school, they also provide curricula for middle and primary school science. DataStudio® is a data collection and analysis software available for both Windows and Macintosh OSs and provides real-time data collection and analysis of the data collected from their various types of sensing probes.

While these examples might provide great potential for learning, not every classroom will have access to these powerful data collection tools. Having limited resources shouldn't limit research learning activities. There are other ways to collect and record data; for example, students can use traditional thermometers to collect temperature, which can then be recorded into a spreadsheet. Perhaps more importantly, data collection shouldn't be limited to simply numerical types of data.

Collecting data with more readily available tools can be utilized to support research and problem-solving learning activities as well. Students can collect still images, videos, and even audio recordings using digital cameras or cell phones. They can measure plant growth in height, but also take a picture of it to illustrate the growth graphically. Or they might narrate verbally on their cell phones the growth that details their observations. Students should be taught to collect and analyze various types of data, using various data collection tools.

Survey Data Collection

Although there are commercial survey tools available, perhaps one of the best tools freely available for collecting survey data is Google Forms. Students can use the "Forms" tool, which is part of the suite of Google Docs to create a survey-style data collection form. Once the form is created it can be sent via email, embedded into a web page on Google Sites, or the URL could simply be shared for others to complete. Form items include questions of various types, such as: multiple choice, true/false, open-ended, ratings, as well as others. As participants complete the survey, data is automatically saved in a Google Docs spreadsheet.

Having students create, disseminate, and collect information in this manner can support research design, data collection, and analysis. Students could email a form to their ePals (2015) in different parts of the country or world asking their peers to provide data on rainfall, temperature, or other quantifiable measures.

Multimedia Data Collection

Digital cameras, iPads, and Android tablets are great devices for gathering sounds, images, and videos, which can support qualitative data collection. In addition, smartphones have become common place in today's classrooms. Although some districts, schools, or teachers have issues with allowing students to use their smartphones in the classroom, these can be great multimedia data collection devices. Data collected in the form of digital files can be shared or sent from the smartphone to a variety of locations or to other devices.

ORGANIZING AND ANALYZING TOOLS

Once data is collected, it needs to be organized and analyzed to draw conclusions on what it might suggest or imply. There are several tools that students can use to do just that, some expensive, some that are freely available. Regardless of the analysis tool, students should practice good file management, storage, organization, security, and safety.

File Storage

While some schools have plenty of storage, there are also free *cloud* storage services for those students who have limited digital storage resources. While there are others, here are three examples: Microsoft OneDrive (2015b), DropBox (2015), and Google Drive (2015b) provide storage that can be directly connected to one's computer or accessed only online. Once an account is created, students have access to free storage, where they can upload and organize their files into folders and subfolders. In addition, most storage services allow for sharing of folders and/or files with others, which supports collaborative projects.

Google Form Data Collection and Analysis

As mentioned before, Google Forms is an excellent tool for students to easily create and disseminate surveys. What might be even more powerful is that as the surveys are submitted, the data is automatically collected into a spreadsheet for analysis. Google Forms has a built-in data summary tool, but the data can also be downloaded to a traditional spreadsheet.

Once the data is available in a spreadsheet it can be viewed from various perspectives and displayed in a graphic manner for analysis that provides a graphic view for the learner. For example, if the results of the sixth-grade ice cream survey were placed in a spreadsheet, a pie chart could be created providing a graphic view of the results as shown in figure 7.1 below.

Today's spreadsheets can house a variety of types of data within each cell, including formulas, which automatically apply mathematical functions such as summing, averaging, etc., to a group of cells. In addition to text and numerical data, most spreadsheets will also allow for multimedia files to be

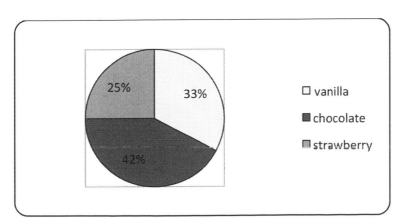

Figure 7.1   Ice Cream Favorites Spreadsheet Graph

inserted as objects, thus allowing students to include images and video and audio files.

InspireData

One commercial tool that is designed specifically to help students in analyzing and organizing quantitative data is InspireData® (2015) and is available for Macintosh and Windows-based computers. InspireData® provides students an easy-to-use data organization and analysis tool with many features. Students can enter their own data, select from various preentered data sets, or import from other data sources, such as a spreadsheet. Data can then be manipulated and viewed in tables or plots, providing students with the opportunity to organize and view it in various ways.

Databases

While similar to a spreadsheet, databases can be used to collect and analyze more complex data. A contacts list on one's phone is an example of a database. A much more complex example would be when one is shopping online. Most online stores use a complex database that allows one to search for a specific element of an item, for example, color, size, etc. Perhaps the most complex database example is Google.

Access (Microsoft, 2015a) and LibreOffice Base (2015) are examples of powerful database programs, which are used by business and industry professionals, as well as educators. There are also some simpler, freely available database programs. One example is Obvibase, which can be added to the Google Suite of applications. It can also save database files directly to one's Google Drive or Dropbox storage areas. Obvibase might be a good option for students who want to get a beginner's understanding of databases.

Helping students use a database program to collect and organize data can be challenging. However, there may be times when this type of application is most appropriate for students, depending on what the lesson objective is and how the tool can best help students.

RESEARCH AND DATA COLLECTION
SCENARIO: PHASES OF THE MOON

Laura is a second-grade teacher who has worked closely with her fellow teachers in implementing a schoolwide inquiry-based science program based upon the Next Generation Science Standards (NGSS) (National Science Teachers Association, 2012). During the planning time, the faculty decided that the second-grade teachers would be responsible for building on the work of the previous grade-level teachers in science inquiry, which is one of the three dimensions of the NGSS Framework. Specifically, the second grade would cover patterns and progressions as they relate to Earth and Space Sciences (ESS).

As a second-grade teacher, Laura would be responsible for helping her students meet the endpoint for grade 2: "Patterns of the motion of the sun, moon, and stars in the sky can be observed, described, and predicted. At night one can see the light coming from many stars with the naked eye, but telescopes make it possible to see many more and to observe them and the moon and planets in greater detail" (p. 174).

She knows that this can be a difficult concept for second graders because what they know about how the earth interacts with other heavenly bodies it is often inferred through personal observation. Since we can only observe the phases of the moon while standing on the earth, we have a limited perspective of this event, causing many to have misconceptions. In other words, if we were in space we would have a better view of the event (Kavanagh et al., 2005). In fact, college students studying to become classroom teachers often still hold science misconceptions they developed early on in their education (Trundle et al., 2007).

Laura decided to design and teach several units throughout the year. The first unit she taught helped her students understand the basic principles of light. Specifically, they learned that light travels in a straight line and that when light strikes an object the side facing the source is lighted and the side facing away from the source remains in the shadow. The next unit would build upon that knowledge to help her students gain an understanding of the phases of the moon. She also wanted to reinforce the NGSS practices of scientific inquiry so she developed the various steps for the unit, which took place over several class periods.

Laura grouped students in teams of three and asked them to utilize Kidspiration® to create a team cognitive map that identified what they knew about the movements of the moon and the earth. Students were then asked to brainstorm things that didn't know, but thought were important to find out about the moon and the earth and to put them into their cognitive map. As Laura moved from team to team, she also encouraged her students to try to come up with these ideas as best they could, providing prompts and guidance as needed.

Each team was then asked to share with the class the things that they thought they knew and the list of things that they wanted to find out. These were projected to the SMART Board® so others could see. With Laura's guidance, the class refined the items that they wanted to find out about into the form of a question to better define the ideas. By developing these "research questions," students could move to the next task, thinking about how they would answer these questions. The refined "research questions" were placed into a new Kidspiration® file that would be given to each team at a later date.

Next, Laura used the SMART Board® and asked the class to brainstorm ideas about how they might answer the research questions. She encouraged them to think about how they could gather information, make personal observations, and use library and online resources to help support their observations. Their ideas were written next to the research questions on the board and refined as Laura structured the discussion.

With Laura's help, the class decided that each student would look at the moon every day to see how it changed. They also decided that it would be a good idea to record what they saw, so Laura also developed an "observation chart." The chart provided images of various moon phases during a complete cycle and a place next to each for students to input the date and time they made their observations.

Students were instructed to ask their parents to help them with their observations. On days when the moon wasn't visible, not visible till too late, or when they weren't able to complete their observations for any other reason, they were asked to predict what they thought the moon might look like and this was marked as a *prediction*. Laura checked with students daily on how the *moon observations* were going, which served as her formative assessment.

After everyone in the class had an opportunity to make their observations throughout the moon's cycle, she created and projected a spreadsheet with the images and dates for each day of the moon phases. She made sure that the spreadsheet was sorted by date to reflect the moon gradually moving through its phases. In addition, Laura again assigned her students into teams where they reviewed and discussed the charts of their teammates.

Laura then gave her students the opportunity to look at library and online resources that she'd previously assembled. Once all of the teams had the opportunity to look over the various resources, each team discussed their ideas and predicted answers to the research questions. Each team used their own copy of the "research questions" Kidspiration® file to enter their predicted answers to the questions in either graphic or text view. Students could then save their predicted answers to be later used for their final report.

Laura explained to the class that their team's predictions were probably accurate, but they would have the opportunity to test them out. Each team was asked to use two balls, of different sizes, and a flashlight to test their ideas of what made the phases of the moon. Students were instructed to think of the flashlight as the sun, the big ball as the earth, and the small ball as the moon. They were to look for evidence in light and shadow that would support their ideas.

They were also provided with digital cameras to take pictures of their prediction-testing activity. She also helped them upload the files to her Google Drive so students could later use them in their reports. Laura checked with each team to see their progress and provided scaffolding when needed, which served as her formative assessment.

As a final activity and a summative assessment, Laura asked each team to create a report that outlined their findings using a presentation software. Teams were encouraged to use the images they took during their hypothesis testing or media that they found from the guided online resources and other resources in their final reports. While students were given the choice to utilize various media in their report, Laura required that each report include a summary or list of the steps of the process that the team went through during their investigation.

Each report needed to have the research questions and the initial predicted answers as they were entered into the team's Kidspiration® file. In addition, each student in the team needed to create their own conclusions slide that described the results of the hypothesis testing and what they thought caused the phases of the moon.

SUMMARY

The purpose of this chapter was to describe how digital tools can be used to help support engaging students in research, data collection, and analysis; inquiry which requires students to do more than simply look up and report information they found on the Internet. Digital tools for research, data collection, and analysis can be used for many disciplines, but are very well suited for instruction using science inquiry.

The scenario for this chapter is a good example of how to integrate digital tools in ways to support original research, even for students as young as second graders. In this case, Laura had to provide a lot of support and scaffolding and had to break down the instruction for her second graders using the SMART Board® and other tools. It is important to remember that depending upon the grade and cognitive level of the students, teachers will need to consider how to adjust their scaffolding when integrating digital tools to support research, data collection, and analysis.

REFERENCES AND RESOURCES

Common Core: State Standards Initiative. (2015). English and Language Arts Standards. Retrieved from: http://www.corestandards.org/ELA-Literacy/.

Common Core: State Standards Initiative. (2015). Mathematics Standards. Retrieved from: http://www.corestandards.org/Math/.

Dropbox. (2015). Dropbox: Good things happen when your stuff lives here. Retrieved from: https://www.dropbox.com/.

Google. (2015a). Google. Retrieved from: http://www.google.com.

Google. (2015b). Google Drive: A safe place for all of your files. Retrieved from: https://www.google.com/intl/en/drive/.

Google. (2015c). Google Forms. Retrieved from: https://www.google.com/forms/about/.

Harris, R. (2013, December 27). *Evaluating Internet Research Sources*. Retrieved from: http://www.virtualsalt.com/evalu8it.htm.

Houghton Mifflin Company. (2015). Using the Web: Finding and Evaluating Web Sites. Retrieved from: http://www.eduplace.com/kids/usingweb/g6-8.html.

Inspiration Software, Inc. (2015). InspireData: The Visual Way to Explorer and Understand Data. Retrieved from: http://www.inspiration.com/InspireData.

Kavanagh, C., Agan, L., and Sneider, C. (2005). Learning about phases of the moon and eclipses: A guide for teachers and curriculum developers. *Astronomy Education Review*, *4* (1), 19–52.

Lewis, A., and Smith, D. (1993). Defining higher order thinking. *Theory into practice*, *32* (3), 131–37.

Microsoft. (2015a). Access. Database software and applications. Retrieved from: https://products.office.com/en-us/access.

Microsoft. (2015b). OneDrive: One place for everything in your life. Retrieved from: https://onedrive.live.com/about/en-us/.

National Science Teachers Association. (2012). Next generation science standards. Retrieved from: http://www.nsta.org/about/standardsupdate/default.aspx.

Obvibase. (2015). Obvibase: A truly simple database. Retrieved from: https://www.obvibase.com/.

Pasco. (2015). DataStudio: 3-Axis Accelerometer/Altimeter. Retrieved from: http://www.pasco.com/prodCatalog/PS/PS-2136_pasport-3-axis-accelerometer-altimeter/index.cfm.

The Document Team. (2015). LibreOffice (Version 5.0.4) [Software]. Available from: http://www.documentfoundation.org/.

Trundle, K. C., Atwood, R. K., and Christopher, J. E. (2007). Fourth-grade elementary students' conceptions of standards-based lunar concepts. *International Journal of Science Education*, *29* (5), 595–616.

Vernier Software and Technology, LLC. (2015). Retrieved from: http://www.vernier.com/.

Chapter 8

Creating and Publishing

When students use digital tools such as Mindtools (Jonassen, 2000), they engage in creative thinking and construct knowledge as they create and publish meaningful artifacts (Resnick, 1996). This chapter will provide examples of how students might use some of these digital tools, such as visualization tools, to help them organize their thoughts by creating a cognitive map that outlines their understanding of a topic. Students can then use publishing tools to create meaningful products as they cement their understandings of that topic.

CREATING AND PUBLISHING

It is easy to think about using Internet tools to gather information and then a word processor or presentation software to produce a document that shows what students can do and what they have learned. However, there are many other technology tools that students can use that go far beyond finding information and compiling it into a document. Let's think about how teachers might integrate technology tools in a complex, student-centered manner.

To learn new information, students need to think about their background knowledge on a topic so that they can then begin to build upon that knowledge or those understandings. Teachers often use a KWL (Know, Want to know, Learned) chart to begin a new lesson to help their students begin to organize and plan their learning. They list (a) what they know about the topic, (b) what they want to learn about the topic, and then (c) go back and review what they learned about the topic. Table 8.1 is an example of a KWL chart, which helps students access and organize their background knowledge and plan out their learning goals for the upcoming lesson.

Table 8.1   KWL Chart

K *What I Already Know* *(Accessing Background* *Knowledge)*	W *What I Want to Know* *(Planning to Learn)*	L *What I Learned* *(Self-Assessment of* *Learning)*

While the KWL chart displayed in table 8.1 provides students the opportunity to organize and plan their learning, there are technology tools that can do similar things that are perhaps more powerful for learning. Students can use visualization tools to help them organize their thoughts by making a cognitive map of what they know about a topic. Once they've listed the things they know, they can then begin to identify the things they don't know by adding their ideas on the map, thus helping them outline what they need to learn.

As they research their topic using a variety of learning resources, they can verify what they know and gather information about the things that they don't know. In doing so, they must figure out how any new information fits into their former understandings. Then, with the help of a publishing tool, students can build upon their knowledge as they construct and assemble meaningful products. By creating meaningful products they are given the opportunity to bring the pieces together to demonstrate their new knowledge and understanding.

VISUALIZATION TOOLS

Students often have difficulties getting their ideas out on paper. Semantic or cognitive mapping has long been a strategy to help them organize their thoughts about a variety of topics, especially in the learning of language arts in elementary and middle school (Heimlich and Pittelman, 1986). While students can create these with pencil and paper, there are several visualization tools that can help support a learner in developing a semantic or cognitive map, such as Kidspiration®, Inspiration® (Inspiration Software, Inc., 2015), and cMap Tools (Institute for Human and Machine Cognition, 2015).

By using a visualization tool, students are supported in creating more dynamic models to help them explore more complex concepts, systems, and/ or issues. As they create their cognitive map, students can organize ideas or concepts *graphically* and think about possible connections between the elements.

Figure 8.1 illustrates how students might use a cognitive mapping tool to organize what they know about a central topic in terms of how the elements are connected to it in various ways. The central topic here is mammals and students can list all the things that they know about mammals. They can also add questions about mammals for which they'd like to find answers. They can graphically visualize the various elements that they think might be part of the central topic and envision additional aspects, which help them generate new ideas about that topic.

Clip arts can be included or images from the Internet can be copied and pasted to help students reflect upon and organize their thoughts about mammals. This view may help students who better visualize the topic in a graphic

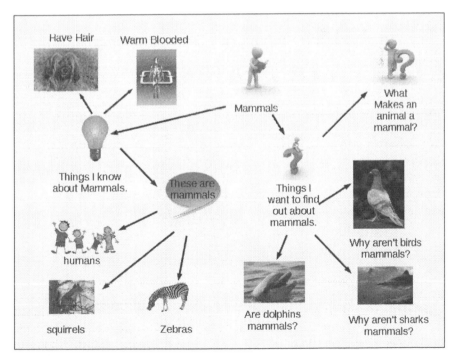

Figure 8.1   Graphic Organizer or Cognitive Map

Textbox 8.1

Mammals

1. Things I know about mammals
   a. Have hair
   b. Are warm-blooded
2. These are mammals
   a. Humans
   b. Zebras
   c. Squirrels
3. Things I want to find out about mammals
   a. What makes an animal a mammal?
   b. Why aren't sharks mammals?
   c. Are dolphins mammals?
   d. Why aren't birds mammals?

organizer, which has been recommended as a strategy to increase comprehension by using a common language (graphics) to better support English language learners (Reed and Railsbeck, 2003).

Perhaps the most powerful aspect of this type of digital visualization tool is that many cognitive mapping tools can easily turn a *graphic organizer* into an *outline* with the click of a mouse. By doing so, students can then see the hierarchical structure, as shown below. Being able to move back and forth between outline and graphic format allows students to view their cognitive map from various perspectives.

Depending upon a student's strength, they can work in either format, graphic or outline, or even switch back and forth between the two. Some visualization tools allow students to export the final outline into a word processor or presentation software to help them better organize their written document or presentation.

PUBLISHING TOOLS

There are several tools to help students construct knowledge as they create meaningful products and demonstrate their thoughts and knowledge in their published documents. Most schools have computer labs or a few computers in each classroom that students use to create many electronic artifacts. Some schools have great digital tools available for their students, while others have fewer. Remember, however, that there are open-source software titles that can help support teachers with fewer resources.

Document Creation

Word processors are often used by students to create documents that can demonstrate their understandings of specific content, as in a science report. Document creation has been shown to boost the writing processes of students with learning disabilities (MacArthur, 1996). There are templates that can be downloaded to enhance word processors into powerful print publishing tools that support students in creating more robust and complex documents. In addition, there are print publishing tools, such as Microsoft Publisher (Microsoft, 2015), that support just about any kind of published product.

Students can use these templates to support their creation of many types of documents, including brochures, flyers, business cards, postcards, and newsletters, to name a few. For example, teachers might encourage the use of the brochure template when their students are creating a volunteer environmental vacation brochure that details information on one of the earth's many global environmental issues. Today's word processors also allow for very complex document formatting that supports more innovative publications such as embedding multimedia, which can enhance products, making a word processor a very powerful publishing tool.

Multimedia Editing and Creation

Multimedia biographies can be developed, where images, audio narratives, and videos are collected and/or created, thus enhancing student engagement and ownership in the learning activity (Jonassen, 2006). By creating an original multimedia artifact, students are given the opportunity for personal or group expression in a more innovative and creative way to demonstrate their knowledge and/or skills through presentations that include images, audio recordings, and videos. Presentation software is usually part of the productivity suites that schools might own or included in open-source software that can be downloaded for free.

Image Creation and Manipulation

OSs include an image creation tool that can be used by students for creating or editing images (e.g., Paint in Windows). Students can use these basic image creation tools to save images in a variety of file formats that can then be embedded or imported into other documents or multimedia presentations. Gimp (The Gimp Team, 2015), an open-source image manipulation software that can be downloaded for free, is a very powerful image creation tool available for both the Macintosh and Windows computers. Images captured using digital cameras or downloaded from the Internet can be manipulated to best suit the student's project.

Audio Creation and Manipulation

OSs also include basic sound recording software. One of the best, free audio creation and manipulation tools is Audacity (2015). It can be downloaded and installed on most OSs, and by using a built-in microphone or adding an inexpensive headset with microphone, can be used to record, import, and edit audio files. Using audio in this fashion may be especially powerful for students with limited writing ability as a way to demonstrate their understanding by describing or narrating their thoughts.

Video Creation and Manipulation

Another powerful way to support student creativity is through video. Most laptop computers come with a camera and microphone that will record video and audio, which make video creation somewhat simple. In addition, students can use a moviemaking program such as Apple's iMovie (2015) and Window's Movie Maker (2015). Although more robust video creation and editing tools are commercially available, Movie Maker and iMovie are quite powerful when used in concert with audio and image editing software. Both can be used to create and edit various media files, including video clips, still images, and audio.

At the heart of Barrett's (2008) work on digital storytelling, she describes how students can use Movie Maker and iMovie to construct digital stories by creating a video that requires them to organize information, write narration, and utilize multimedia. In addition to utilizing advanced multimedia tools to edit audio, images, and video, digital storytelling provides students with the opportunity to create a portfolio element that demonstrates their understanding and reflects upon on their learning experience as they construct their meaningful product.

E-books

E-books created by students is another great way to demonstrate their understandings, and especially their literacy—in both writing and technology. An e-book provides an excellent digital artifact that requires learners to demonstrate their skills at writing, layout, design, and creativity as well.

Apple provides a free authoring tool called iBook Author (Apple, 2015), which, when completed, can be read on an iPad or a computer with the latest Macintosh OS. It is quite powerful, yet easy to learn and provides the opportunity for students to demonstrate their writing and also supports embedding a variety of media, including images, audio, and video. Students can also save an iBook Author file in PDF format, which allows for greater flexibility in sharing their work with those who do not have access to an iPad or Macintosh computer.

There are many other e-book authoring applications for both the iPad and Android-based tablets—some more powerful than others. In addition, some word processors also have ePub (electronic publication) plug-ins, allowing to save a document created in the *ePub* format, which can be read by many tablets and smartphones. While this is a more affordable option if teachers don't have the resources, it is wise that they try these tools out prior to having their students work with them. There are quite a few applications and plug-ins available that can be difficult to work with and could be very frustrating for students.

SHARING PUBLISHED WORKS

Students will also benefit from sharing their newly acquired knowledge through a presentation to the class, which is an example of technology integration at a Type II application level (Maddux et al., 2001). Certainly, social media has provided a variety of venues for students to present and share their work. While care does have to be taken when publishing to the general public, access can be limited to a safe, but broader audience, such as ePals, which helps teachers connect students in other schools and other countries (ePals, 2015).

Social Media

Social media has quickly become the most common way to share thoughts, activities, photos, videos, and a variety of other elements of our lives. For example, Facebook provides a venue for one to share just about every aspect of one's life. In addition, Twitter provides instant access to one's thoughts in 140 characters. While these applications are very popular and there are ways to integrate these into the classroom, there are other tools that might better serve for classroom publishing.

Wikis and blogs are Internet-based applications that permit students to individually or collaboratively publish their research. However, these tools also permit embedding images, audio files, and videos, thus making them multimedia creation tools.

YouTube, podcasts, and vodcasts are publishing tools that are audio-video based. Podcasts are audio recordings in MP3 file format and can be listened to on an Apple iPod or directly from the Internet. By adding video, students can create their own VidCast or vodcast (video podcasts). Vodcasts, like podcasts, are watched on a video-enabled iPod or directly from the Internet.

Student-created podcasts or vodcasts can then be attached to discussion board postings, sent through email, or embedded within a blog or wiki to provide additional opportunities for students to publish their multimedia products. Doing so helps them communicate their ideas and information to a variety of audiences utilizing various media and formats.

Web-Based Publication

Using Google Sites (Google, 2015) students can easily create a website where they publish their work and share it with a wider audience. Access to the site can be limited to only those invited or made public to everyone. In addition, Google Sites, like all Google features, supports collaboration where students can coauthor a site regardless of where they are in the world. Google Sites also supports multimedia so that files can be attached for sharing.

iPads, Tablets, and e-Readers

If students intend to share their e-books, it's important to know that there are several file formats, which can be read only by specific e-readers. For example, the Kindle, generally uses the *mobi* format, while other software might use *ePub*. Therefore, it is wise to become familiar with the various file formats, readers, and tools that are available. However, e-reader app for phones and tablets for the various e-book file formats can generally be downloaded for free.

Sharing an electronic book can be done in a variety of ways. Calibre (2015) is an open-source electronic library management tool that can be downloaded on a computer connected to the Internet that allows users to access the e-books stored there. In addition, Calibre can be used to convert e-books from one format to another, which is a great feature as many e-book readers need e-books to be in specific file formats. Calibre's online electronic library also provides for access control, so the sharing of the e-books can be limited, and thereby protected, or open to the general public.

SCENARIO: LANGUAGE ARTS PUBLISHING—HERO'S JOURNEY

Bill is a fourth-grade language arts teacher who wants his students to achieve the Common Core ELA Standards "Reading: Literature" and "Writing." Specifically, being able to read and understand key ideas and details (CCSS. ELA-Literacy.RL.4.1, CCSS.ELA-Literacy.RL.4.2, and CCSS.ELA-Literacy.RL.4.3) and being able to produce and distribute writing (CCSS.ELA-Literacy.W.4.6) (Common Core ELA, 2015).

Bill decides that he wants to use *The Hero with a Thousand Faces* (Campbell, 2008) as the foundation for his unit where his students would read about the Hero's Journey and then identify a person who they thought was a hero based upon their understanding of what they read. He also wants to integrate technology in such a way as to allow his students work together to construct team products that demonstrate their individual creativity but also their ability to collaborate. Students would use Google Sites to create a website that provides the details of their hero, which includes a rationale as to why he or she is their hero.

Bill decides that he wants his students to work in teams, but also wants to ensure that each student is held accountable for meeting the language arts and technology outcomes. Therefore, he designs the unit with a variety of ways to assess the students work. Specifically, each team will focus on a specific category of person from the past (i.e., no longer living); this could be (a) an author, (b) a scientist or inventor, (c) an artist, (d) a historical or political figure, (e) a sports figure, or (f) a service figure (i.e., fireman, policeman, member of the armed forces, etc.).

Each member of the team will have to identify, research, and report on his or her individual hero within the team's category. Once all of the teams finish their websites, each student will review their peers' work and post comments within the comments section. Bill knows that this can be tricky, so he gives good instructions on how the comments should be positive and constructive. In addition, students know that because the Google Sites are not open to the public, each one must log in and the author's name will appear in the comments.

Bill has six computers in his classroom that are fairly new, have an office suite, video editing software, and Internet connectivity. In addition, his students are scheduled to go to the school computer lab for two class periods each week. He's discussed the unit with the person in charge of the building's technology support, who shared with Bill that the computers in the lab would work very well for his students' projects since they each have a built-in camera and video editing software, and the lab also has headsets with microphones that students can check out.

Bill believes that his students will have the technology that will support them in creating final projects that include the following elements and structure. Each team will use Google Sites to create a website that will have (a) a title page, (b) an overview of their category of heroes, (c) a menu that links to each member's individual area of the website, and (d) an area for comments.

Each member's area can include various web pages or an embedded presentation (i.e., PowerPoint, or Prezi) that includes the following: (a) an introduction of their chosen hero that includes the details of who, what, when, and where; and (b) a rationale that explains why this person should be considered a hero, based upon the twelve stages or steps of the Hero's Journey outlined by Campbell. Each team member's contribution should include images, audio files, and videos (i.e., Internet-acquired media) that help detail their hero's journey and/or their rationale for why they chose that individual (through video interview or audio narration).

Bill then outlines the criteria that he will use for his summative assessment. Using the fourth-grade-level Common Core ELA for Reading: Literature and Writing, he creates a rubric to help him assess his students' work.

For Reading: Literature, he creates a row for each of the following: "CCSS.ELA-Literacy.RL.4.1: Refer to details and examples in a text when explaining what the text says explicitly and when drawing inferences from the text. CCSS.ELA-Literacy.RL.4.2: Determine a theme of a story, drama, or poem from details in the text; summarize the text. CCSS.ELA-Literacy. RL.4.3: Describe in depth a character, setting, or event in a story or drama, drawing on specific details in the text (e.g., a character's thoughts, words, or actions)" (Common Core: State Standards Initiative, 2015, p. 12).

He also includes a row for the Writing outcomes for "CCSS.ELA-Literacy.W.4.6: Production and Distribution of Writing. With some guidance and support from adults, use technology, including the Internet, to produce and publish writing as well as to interact and collaborate with others; demonstrate sufficient command of keyboarding skills to type a minimum of one page in a single sitting" (Common Core: State Standards Initiative, 2015, p. 21).

Bill also knows that he will need to create a formative assessment plan, and that he should be flexible in making sure that he gives his students enough time, opportunity, resources, and scaffolding to be successful in this unit. He begins by organizing a time frame for what he thinks it will take and breaks that down into class periods. However, he also knows that he will need to keep a close watch and take notes of the students' use of technology and how well they work in teams. These close observations and anecdotal notes will help him and his students monitor their progress and adjust for difficulties they might have.

Bill believes he should provide some greater structure and decides that each team should first develop a mind map. So, he encourages each team to use Inspiration to create a mind map, which will serve as a graphic organizer for their websites. He knows that working together on the team's mind map will not only help students make decisions and organize their project, but it will also help them understand that it is a plan, which may need adjustments as they begin to work on it.

He also requires each student to use Inspiration to create their own mind map. He explains that the purpose of the individual mind map will help them identify what they know about their chosen hero and what they need to find out, and that they can also list links to resources and media that they will need when they begin to develop their individual task. He again reminds them that it is a plan, which may need to be amended.

By requiring each team and individual to create the Inspiration mind map, he can use these as formative assessment items. He can observe and assess team interactions such as team organization, role assignment, and identifying individual heroes. When he finds that a team is having difficulties during the development of the mind maps, he can provide team coaching to help them identify and assign task roles. Likewise, if he finds an individual having difficulties, he can provide coaching to help that student structure and organize his or her individual area of the website.

While the mind maps will provide a formative assessment element, he also wants to encourage self-monitoring. He creates a checklist for each member that outlines all of the various elements of structure that are expected for the individual areas and explains that they should use this to ensure that their area isn't missing any of the requirements. By providing these scaffolds and having students keep track of their progress in this manner, they have a better chance of being successful.

SUMMARY

The focus of this chapter was to provide an overview of how students might construct knowledge with the help of visualization and publishing tools in the creation and sharing of meaningful artifacts or products. The chapter provided examples of digital tools that support the creation of documents, e-books, websites, and multimedia. It also provided examples of how students might present or share their work through a variety of technology tools designed to help them publish their work.

Designing lessons that integrate technology to support student creativity and publishing requires some imagination. The scenario presented in this chapter went beyond simply researching information on the Internet and having students report back their findings. Rather, the chapter provided examples of using visualization tools to help students access and organize their background knowledge. The scenario also described how the teacher planned formative assessment items and scaffolds to support his students' success with this unit. These are important elements when planning a complex unit using creation and publishing tools.

REFERENCES AND RESOURCES

Apple (2015). iBook Author. Retrieved from: http://www.apple.com/.
Audacity (2008). Audacity: Free audio editor and recorder. Retrieved from: http://audacity.sourceforge.net/.

Barrett, H. (2006). *Digital storytelling tools.* Retrieved from: http://electronicportfo-lios.com/digistory/tools.html.

Calibre (2015). E-Book Management. Retrieved from: http://calibre-ebook.com/.

Campbell, J. (2008). *The hero with a thousand faces* (vol. 17). Navato, CA: New World Library.

Common Core: State Standards Initiative. (2015). *English and Language Arts Standards.* Retrieved from: http://www.corestandards.org/ELA-Literacy/.

ePals (2015). Where learners connect. Retrieved from: http://www.epals.com/.

Google.com. (2015). *Google Docs: Create and edit documents online, for free.* Retrieved from: https://www.google.com/docs/about/.

Heimlich and Pittelman. (1986). *Semantic Mapping: Classroom Applications. Reading Aids Series*, IRA Service Bulletin, Book No. 230. Newark, DE: International Reading Association.

Inspiration Software, Inc. (2008). Inspiration. Retrieved from: http://www.inspiration.com.

Institute for Human and Machine Cognition. (2015). *cMap Tools.* Retrieved from: http://cmap.ihmc.us\.

Jonassen, D. (2006). *Modeling with technology: Mindtools for conceptual change.* third ed. Upper Saddle River, NJ: Merrill Prentice Hall.

Jonassen, D. H. (2000). *Computers as mindtools for schools: Engaging critical thinking.* second ed. Upper Saddle River, NJ: Merrill Prentice Hall.

MacArthur, C. A., (1996). Using technology to enhance the writing processes of students with learning disabilities. *Journal of Learning Disabilities, 29* (4), 344–54.

Maddux, C. C., Johnson, D. L., and Willis, J. W. (2001). *Educational Computing: Learning with tomorrow's technologies,* third ed. Needham Heights, MA: Allyn & Bacon.

Microsoft. (2015). Movie Maker. Retrieved from: http://windows.microsoft.com/en-US/windows-live/movie-maker.

Microsoft. (2016). Publisher. Retrieved from: https://products.office.com/en-us/publisher.

National Council of Teachers of English (NCTE) and the International Reading Association (IRA). (2015). *Standards for the English language arts.* Retrieved from: http://www.ncte.org/standards/ncte-ira.

Reed, B. and Railsbeck, J. (2003). *Strategies and resources for mainstream teachers of English language learners.* Retrieved August 11, 2008, from: http://www.nwrel.org/request/2003may/ell.pdf.

Resnick, M. (1996). *Distributed constructionism.* In Proceedings of the 1996 international conference on learning sciences (pp. 280–84). Evanston, IL: International Society of the Learning Sciences.

The Document Foundation. (2015). LibreOffice: Home—Free office suite. Retrieved from: https://www.libreoffice.org/.

The Gimp Team. (2014). Gimp—The GNU image manipulation program. Retrieved from: http://www.gimp.org/.

Chapter 9

Thinking Critically

Solving Problems and Making Decisions

Through visual representations, today's digital tools and educational software can provide opportunities for students to examine, investigate, practice, or explore activities, which might be dangerous, expensive, difficult, or simply impossible for students. By using case-based, project-based, inquiry-based, and problem-based learning strategies, teachers can engage their students in ways that support learning at a deeper level of critical thinking, problem-solving, and decision-making.

This chapter will provide examples of using digital tools to support students as they begin to tackle real-life issues and problems. Through the integration of simulations, scenarios, exploratory, and logical thinking tools, students can practice, explore, and manipulate complex concepts and try out their ideas in a safe environment, which helps them gain a more accurate understanding of things.

CRITICAL THINKING, PROBLEM-SOLVING, AND DECISION-MAKING

Making knowledgeable decisions that help solve real-world problems requires that one be able to explore and identify various solutions from a variety of perspectives. To help students learn these skills, teachers have used case-based, project-based, inquiry-based, or a problem-based instructional strategies where students are engaged in research of some kind, analyzing findings, and applying their knowledge and skills to visualize solutions and make decisions.

The general difference between these instructional strategies is how the teacher structures the learning environment in terms of responsibility for learning. Depending upon grade level, cognitive abilities, and the specific instructional strategy employed, the teacher may provide more or less structure. A problem-based learning activity may only provide an "ill-structured" problem requiring students to organize and control all aspects of the activity. When employing a project-based unit, the teacher might provide roles with specific tasks, step-by-step instructions for the process, and detailed instructions for students to follow.

Using an instructional strategy that provides less structure gives students more control for learning decisions, and requires them to think more critically, organize more thoroughly, solve problems as they arise, and make decisions—that is, carry out all aspects of the learning process. Using an instructional strategy that provides greater structure supports students who may not be ready or able to do all those things. Selecting the appropriate instructional strategy should be based upon the students. However, it's important to help them take more control of the learning process in these strategies so they can begin to gain these higher-order thinking skills.

TOOLS FOR EXPLORATION

There are instructional strategies and educational software programs that provide opportunities to enhance critical thinking, problem-solving, and decision-making, which foster higher-order thinking skills. These tools can provide a safe virtual environment where students can learn in ways that allow them to investigate concepts, manipulate variables, and try out their ideas. By integrating scenarios and simulations, teachers can support their students' exploration of ideas, concepts, and methods.

Scenarios

Creating a scenario can provide structured support for project-based learning. This does not mean that these are digital scenarios, but rather that students use digital tools to investigate and create final products for the scenario. A quick Internet search for two classic scenarios, Dream Vacation and Travel Agent, will yield some great lesson and unit plans that integrate a variety of subjects.

In the Dream Vacation scenario, students are given the task of planning a vacation where they must design an itinerary and gather information that includes cost for transportation, housing, food, and entertainment. Students gather other information, such as local events, historical sites, geographical elements, weather, and/or demographics (depending upon how the teacher wants to integrate these subjects). Often, students are also required to create a budget spreadsheet.

In the Travel Agent scenario, students conduct similar searches, but use a digital publishing tool to create an advertisement brochure, a website, or video commercial that includes all of the required information. Students engage in Internet searches to gather information and media, which is then put into some form of digitally published advertisement.

These are just two examples that have been used by many teachers. However, it's important to remember that the key to designing a good scenario lies in how well the students are engaged in the *process* of thinking critically to investigate issues, make decisions, and solve problems, and not in just creating a cool final product. There are many online resources for integrating scenarios into the classroom, including "Scenario-Based Learning" (Wiki-Educator, 2011), "How to Engage Learners with Scenario-Based Learning" (Kovi and Spiro, 2013), and "Three Ways to Use Scenarios" (Bean, 2010).

Simulations

Simulations are virtual settings that allow students to explore and try out ideas, concepts, and skills that might otherwise be too expensive or possibly dangerous. The classic simulation is the computerized flight simulator that allows students to try flying a plane—without injury upon crashing. Another classic is the online frog dissection. Indeed, there are quite a few virtual labs available that provide a variety of simulations for biology, chemistry, and other subjects. Although many require a paid subscription, there are also free virtual labs and a quick Internet search will provide some great resources.

In addition to the variety of virtual labs, there are other types of digital simulations, which provide digital exploration. Geometer's Sketchpad (McGraw-Hill Education, 2014) is a good example. It is an educational software program (available for PC, MAC, and online) that students can use to explore geometric theorems.

Students often find it difficult to understand how, in Euclidean geometry, the sum of the angles of a triangle always equal 180 degrees. Because the tool allows the user to manipulate the graphic, students can grab and drag one of the corners of the triangle, thus changing the angles, however, the total still always equals 180 degrees. By being able to manipulate triangles in this way, students can engage in a much more concrete exploration of this concept of geometry, physically manipulating and then visually seeing the results, which provide images that help meaning-making within the learning of mathematics (Furner and Marinas, 2007).

Students using these types of digital tools are given the opportunity to explore ideas and concepts and develop and try out models. In doing so, they can virtually see examples of constructs that without those tools must be conceptually visualized. In this way, students begin to construct their

understandings of complex concepts and ideas with the help of more concrete manipulative visual representations that might otherwise require more
formalized operational cognitive development (Piaget, 1976).

By using a simulation to explore concepts or ideas, students are able to
make decisions, control variables, and see the results. They are able to compare, and contrast how changing a variable might influence or impact an
element or situation, giving them the opportunity to make decisions and see
the results. If the results are not favorable, they can remake the decisions to
see how things might change, thus learning safely from their mistakes. There
are several online resources that support using simulations in the classroom,
including Teaching with Simulations (Blecha, 2013) and Use Simulations to
Help Students Learn (Creativeteachingsite.com, 2011).

TOOLS FOR LOGICAL THINKING

Designed in 1967 by Wally Feurzeig and Seymour Papert, LOGO (Chakraborty
et al., 1999) was originally a drawing program that gave students the opportunity to write code that would direct movements of an object, called the
"turtle," which would then be traced with pen and paper. LOGO was then
improved allowing students to design the path that the turtle would take
around the computer screen by writing specific computer programming commands. The purpose was to use computer programs to help students learn by
first figuring out the path they wanted the turtle to take and then convert that
into computer programming language.

Although newer computer applications have become much more sophisticated, many still use similar programs and programming languages. Turtle
Academy (2015) is a free interactive website that teaches programming principles to children across the globe. MathPlayground's (2014) interactive math
programming website provides a LOGO game that allows students to write
code to move the turtle around the screen. There are examples that students
can copy and paste into the command line to see how the program works.
Students can then explore how LOGO works using their own commands.

The MIT Education Arcade (Scheller Teacher Education Program, 2015)
provides a variety of educational resources, including free games, simulations, and digital tools designed to help students build math and science skills.
StarLOGO TNG (MIT STEP, 2015), a visual programming environment
for games and simulations, was developed on the principles of the original
LOGO but uses a 3D graphical interface. This interface allows students to
see and explore the concepts of simulations and complex systems through
drag-and-drop methods rather than abstract written commands of previous
computer programming languages.

SCENARIO: CRITICAL THINKING, PROBLEM-SOLVING, AND DECISION-MAKING—5TII STREET OVERPASS

John is a fourth-grade teacher at the Oak Street Elementary School. When the school was built, Oak Street was a neighborhood street with little traffic. In the past few years 5th Street, the intersecting street near the school, has become a high traffic thoroughfare, making it hazardous for students crossing the nearby Oak Street and 5th Street intersection. Mrs. Smith, the principal at Oak Street Elementary attended the city council meeting to see what might be done to help alleviate this danger to her students. She was told that the city would need to have evidence and a suggested solution that there was possible danger.

After Mrs. Smith shared that information with her faculty, John suggested that this might be just the opportunity for the unit he was designing for a College, Career and Civic Life (C3) Framework for Social Studies State Standard. In particular, his unit was to help his fourth graders meet Dimension 4: Taking Informed Action, specifically, D4.8.3-5, where students "use a range of deliberative and democratic procedures to make decisions about and act on civic problems in their classrooms and schools" (p. 62, NCSS, 2013). Mrs. Smith, thinking that it was a great idea, offered any help she could provide.

In designing the unit, John decided that this might be a great way to try out problem-based learning as an instructional strategy. Because he had not tried it with his fourth graders before, he was a bit worried about how it might go. He decided to plan it in such a way that he would give the students a lot of responsibility for trying to solve this problem, but would also provide support in terms of scaffolds and/or structure as they progressed.

To assess the unit, John decided that students would create a personal blog. Acting as an electronic journal, each student was required to make an entry about the project from beginning to end. Each day, John provided a journal entry sentence starter to help the students write their reflections. In addition, to ensure that he could keep track of his students' progress in terms of a formative assessment, he created his own blog to write personal reflections and observational anecdotal notes based upon the project, events, and observations.

To begin, John asked his students if they felt safe crossing the intersection of Oak and 5th Street. Most said that it was scary and that a couple of times they saw Mr. Johnson, the crossing guard, get upset with cars that didn't stop for him to allow students to cross. Next, he asked them what they thought might be done. After listening to several ideas, John asked if any of the students had seen the overpass that was built on High Street above the rail road tracks. Most said yes, and then they realized that this might be a way to solve the problem. The city could build an overpass for 5th Street so the students wouldn't have to cross at the intersection any more.

John then explained about Mrs. Smith going to the city council meeting and that they needed to gather information that provided evidence and a possible solution for the problem. He asked the students what information might help provide the evidence. Then he asked, "Do you think it would help to know exactly how many cars go through the intersection during the day?" They all agreed, so John then said. "The city uses a company that sets up traffic counters for projects like this and if we go to the city council meeting and present our ideas, they might agree to do that on both Oak and 5th Street, which would gather the information we might need."

John asked his students if they thought that creating a presentation of pictures or videos that showed all of the traffic would help convince the city council to hire the car counting company. One of the students, Charity, suggested that she could use her phone to take pictures and videos of the cars on her way to school. Other students said that they too could do the same. Over the next week, the students took pictures and videos of the traffic at the intersection and created a presentation that they then gave to the city council at their next meeting.

At the meeting, the council members said that they were impressed with the presentation and they agreed that the issue should be studied in more detail. They agreed to set up a traffic counter to gather data that would detail not only how much traffic there was, but also show the time and days of heaviest traffic. They also decided that if the students would present a proposal that analyzed the data to see if the heaviest traffic was during the times when they needed to cross the intersection and then suggest some ideas on how to make the intersection safer for them, they would consider their proposal.

Once the traffic counter was in place, it didn't take too long for John to get the data from the city council. He then told the students that they had been given the problem of trying to figure out the busiest day and time for the traffic at the intersection of Oak Street and 5th Street. John helped the students view the data in a spreadsheet. Table 9.1 indicates the number of vehicles that travel through an intersection during different times of the day for each day of the week.

While the numerical values helped his students get an idea of the busiest time and day, a line chart provided a different and more graphic view. By having both the numbers listed and the graphic view, John's students could view the data from two different perspectives. Table 9.1 displays the specific number of vehicles at different times on each day of the week, but the graph in figure 9.1 helped his students better see the spikes in traffic at different times of the day.

Looking at the information from a graphic perspective helped John's students see that the mornings, when students were crossing the intersection, was the busiest time of traffic for every day of the week. In addition, they also

Table 9.1   5th and Oak Street Traffic Table

Hour of the day	Day of the week						
	Monday	Tuesday	Wednesday	Thursday	Friday	Saturday	Sunday
6:00–7:00 AM	1250	1189	1268	1154	1097	507	451
7:00–8:00 AM	2536	2621	2489	2566	2378	789	655
8:00–9:00 AM	2835	2921	2879	2854	2745	1025	1206
9:00–10:00 AM	2206	2342	2251	2301	2160	1209	1248
10:00–11:00 AM	1852	1875	1862	1840	1798	1464	1255
11:00–12:00 AM	1799	1821	1841	1865	1812	1658	1426
12:00–1:00 PM	2644	2732	2711	2659	2589	1743	1654
1:00–2:00 PM	2106	2158	2134	2169	2074	1894	1785
2:00–3:00 PM	1735	1752	1788	1744	1689	1854	1798
3:00–4:00 PM	1862	1895	1877	1853	1822	1821	1625
4:00–5:00 PM	2099	2154	2169	2184	2106	1833	1648
5:00–6:00 PM	2932	2984	3021	3042	3151	2015	1612
6:00–7:00 PM	2564	2622	2612	2586	2851	1432	1095
Total	28420	29066	28902	28817	28272	19244	17458
Average	2186.15	2235.85	2223.23	2216.69	2174.77	1480.31	1342.92

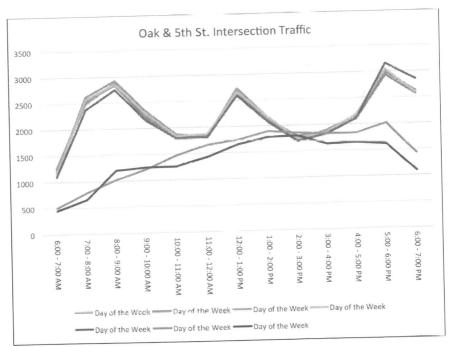

Figure 9.1   Graphic View of 5th and Oak Street Traffic

realized that the time around noon was also a heavy traffic time, just when the morning kindergartners were going home and the afternoon kindergartners were coming to school. The students realized that this information could be used as evidence when presenting their proposal to the city council and set about creating it.

John was able to set up another time for the students to attend the city council to present their proposal. They presented their evidence of the high traffic times coinciding with students crossing the intersection in the mornings and at noon and suggested that an overpass be built for the traffic on 5th Street. The council members agreed that the evidence was compelling, but that the cost of an overpass was very expensive and would delay traffic quite a bit during the construction. In addition, they said that the traffic during the 2:30–3:30 p.m. time period, when students were walking home, wasn't as heavy.

Given the cost and amount of afternoon traffic, the council members asked the students if they could think of another solution. Billy, one of the more quiet students, said, "What if you built an overpass for us?" The council members thought for a moment and then said that this was a great idea. A pedestrian overpass would cost a fraction of one constructed for vehicles and could be done without as much construction impact on traffic and in less time. And although the traffic isn't as heavy during the afternoon times, it would provide a safe walkway for students going home. The city council agreed to open the project up for bids.

SUMMARY

The purpose of this chapter was to provide examples of various digital tools that students can use to support their critical thinking, problem-solving, and decision-making. Integrating these digital tools was described from mostly a student-centered perspective. Teachers need to decide whether to provide more or less structure depending upon the grade level, instructional strategy implemented, and cognitive abilities of their students.

In providing less structure, students will have more control and responsibility, and the teacher will be required to provide appropriate scaffolds as needed. Doing so requires the teachers to relinquish the control and responsibility of learning to the students. The chapter also included examples of digital tools used for exploration and logical thinking, including scenarios and simulations, which provide context.

While the scenario for this chapter was problem-based in nature, it also included a great deal of teacher-provided scaffolds for the students as they went through the unit. In particular, John designed the unit where he could guide his students by providing thought-provoking questions and suggestions.

By doing so, he supported his students' creative thinking, problem-solving, and decision-making from various perspectives in meeting C3 Dimension 4: D4.8.3–5, where students "use a range of deliberative and democratic procedures to make decisions about and act on civic problems in their classrooms and schools."

John had his students make use of several digital tools to gather, manipulate, and analyze both quantitative and qualitative data. First, he supported their use of phones to capture pictures and videos. Next, he helped them organize two presentations, including one that embedded multimedia to present their initial idea to the city council. Next, he helped them use a spreadsheet to view data in both numerically specific and graphic ways, which allowed his students to analyze the data from multiple perspectives. Finally, he helped them create another presentation to present their evidence supported by their data analysis findings.

REFERENCES AND RESOURCES

Bean, C. (2010). Kineo. City and Guilds Group. *Three Ways to Use Scenarios*. Retrieved from: http://www.kineo.com/us/resources/top-tips/learning-strategy-and-design/three-ways-to-use-scenarios.

Blecha, B. (2013). Teaching with Simulations, *Pedagogy in Action*. Retrieved from: http://serc.carleton.edu/sp/library/simulations/index.html.

Chakraborty, A., Graebner, R., and Stocky, T. (1999). *Logo: A project history*. Retrieved from: http://web.mit.edu/6.933/www/LogoFinalPaper.pdf.

CreativeTeachingSite.Com. (2011). Educational Simulations: Use Simulations To Help Students Learn. Retrieved from: http://www.creativeteachingsite.com/edusims.html.

Furner, J. M., and Marinas, C. A. (2007). Geometry sketching software for elementary children: Easy as 1, 2, 3. *Eurasia Journal of Mathematics, Science & Technology Education*, *3* (1), 83–91.

Kovi, H. and Spiro, K. (2013). Learning Solutions Magazine. Focus Media, Inc. *How to Engage learners with Scenario-Based Learning*. Retrieved from: http://www.learningsolutionsmag.com/articles/1108/how-to-engage-learners-with-scenario-based-learning-.

MathPlayground.com. (2014). Math Programming. Retrieved from: http://www.mathplayground.com/mathprogramming.html.

McGraw-Hill Education. (2014). Geometer's Sketchpad. Retrieved from: http://www.dynamicgeometry.com/.

MIT STEP. (2015). StarLogo TNG. *Massachusetts Institute of Technology: Scheller Teacher Education Program*. Retrieved from: http://education.mit.edu/projects/starlogo-tng.

National Council for the Social Studies (NCSS), The College, Career, and Civic Life (C3) Framework for Social Studies State Standards: Guidance for Enhancing the

Rigor of K–12 Civics, Economics, Geography, and History (Silver Spring, MD: NCSS, 2013).

Piaget, J. (1976). Piaget's theory (pp. 11–23). New York: Springer Berlin Heidelberg.

Scheller Teacher Education Program. (2015). MIT Education Arcade. Retrieved from: http://education.mit.edu/.

TurtleAcademy. (2015). Learn LOGO Programing in Your Browser. Retrieved from: https://turtleacademy.com/.

WikiEducator. (2011). Scenario Based Learning. Retrieved from: http://wikieducator.org/Scenario_Based_Learning.

Chapter 10

Digital Games for Learning

Educational software publishers realized and have been taking advantage of the motivational aspect of including gaming elements in their software for decades. An old example, Oregon Trail (Houghton Mifflin Harcourt, 2015), allows students to "win" by surviving the virtual journey, and the *hunting for food* action element is similar to the first-person shooter video games of today. The chapter sheds light on the various types of games and the impact gaming has on learning and also provides some ideas of how to take advantage of the motivation and benefits that it may offer when integrated into classroom learning.

DIGITAL GAMES FOR LEARNING

There are a variety of video games and there are many ways to integrate them into a classroom, therefore it's important to understand how each might impact students. Teachers should be knowledgeable about how to take advantage of the motivation and benefits a game may offer, but at the same time know how the game can *safely* support their learning objectives. Will the game be for exploring a new concept, practicing skills, or to support higher-order learning such as critical thinking, problem-solving, and decision-making? Are there issues with game play in the classroom?

ISSUES OF GAME PLAY

Mainstream media has published articles that not only outline the benefits of game play in learning, but also the risks or detriments of video gaming. The research suggests that the effects of game play are more complex and its impact is often dependent upon video types, a player's interests, and the behaviors being investigated (Bavelier et al., 2011).

There is some evidence of excessive gaming being correlated to aggressive and potentially addictive behavior, especially in adolescents (Grüsser et al., 2006). Others are convinced that violent video game play creates a risk factor for violent behavior and public policy should focus on how to best deal with that (Anderson et al., 2010). However, Yousafzai et al. (2013) stated that like a gambling addiction, a technology addiction might manifest in different ways. For example, some gamblers might be addicted to casinos, but have no interest in betting on horses. Likewise, some gamers might be addicted to first person shooter games, but have no interest in strategy games.

Although there may be issues with game play in the classroom, there may also be merit to motivating students to engage in a learning activity. However, it is important that game play in the classroom should also have an academic purpose, a rationale, and intentionality.

In addition, it is important to be judicious in game choices as some games can carry added issues. Schwartz (2014) details a social studies teacher, who states that using Skyrim (Bethesda Softworks LLC, 2015) produces rich discussions and enhances the thinking level of his students. However, Skyrim is a role-playing game that includes adult themes such as blood, gore, violence, sex, and alcohol. While this might work very well for this teacher, the students in his classroom, and within his particular school and district, it could very easily be an issue for many parents.

GAME-BASED LEARNING

There are, however, many who believe that game-based learning can motivate and engage students in fun and challenging ways, but it should have some element of entertainment (Dai and Wind, 2011). Some educational experts describe it from a more student-centered approach and suggest that teachers think about their students *playing* and *learning* rather than being entertained (Resnick, 2004). Still others, while they agree with the value of game-based learning, also suggest the need for structure, guidance, direction, and/or scaffolding during instruction (Kirschner et al., 2006; Mayer, 2004; Klahr and Nigam, 2004).

Van Eck (2009) describes using commercial, off-the-shelf games for learning and outlines the notion of game-based learning, providing five philosophical premises:

1. The teacher is technologically competent and assumes the roles of a designer, manager, and facilitator.

2. The student actively engages in the learning process, assumes the role of researcher, and becomes technologically competent.
3. The computer is used as a tool, as it is in the workplace, to enhance learning through the use of real-world data to solve problems.
4. The lesson is student-centered, problem-based, and authentic, and technology is an integral component.
5. The environment incorporates multiple resource-rich activities.

GAME-BASED LEARNING RESOURCES

- 10 Ways Teachers Are Using MMORPGs in the Classroom: http://www. teachthought.com/trending/10-ways-teachers-are-using-mmorpgs-in-the-classroom/.
- Educational Games for Children: http://www.abcya.com/
- Game-Based Learning: http://www.edwcb.net/gaming
- Game-Based Learning Units for the Everyday Teacher: http://www.edutopia.org/blog/video-game-model-unit-andrew-miller
- How Online Simulations Work in the Classroom: http://www.edutopia.org/online-simulations-classroom
- How to Plan Instruction Using the Video Game Model: http://www.edutopia.org/blog/how-to-plan-instruction-video-game-model-judy-willis-md
- MinecraftEdu provides products and services that make it easy for educators to use Minecraft in the classroom. http://minecraftedu.com/about

GAME TYPES

Some people believe that games fall into two categories, education or entertainment, with some being somewhere in the middle—edutainment. The gaming industry describes four general categories: action, role-playing, strategy, and simulations. However, many games often have elements of each.

Action Games

Popular *entertainment* action games are often based on a story line where the player must pay close attention and use quick reflexes if they are to be successful in achieving the goals of the game. Action games are often called "first-person shooter" games, because the goal of the game is to kill or destroy as many virtual enemies or threats as possible. The view is from the "first person's" weapon and players use a gaming controller to move through the game environment, point at, and then shoot the enemies as they appear on the screen.

Researchers cite benefits of playing action games that include enhanced vision and speed of cognitive processing. However, playing a lot of action games might also have some negative effects. For example, because there is so much action, visual attention could be reduced or distracted, which might impact a student's ability to follow information that doesn't move as quickly, like paying attention to the teacher in class (Bavelier et al., 2011).

Action games allow players to play in multiplayer environments and must use communication and collaboration skills to team up and play against other teams using a variety of weaponry. Players must work on their collaboration strategies, decision-making, and critical thinking skills to figure out how they will beat their opponents. To help students transfer those skills into productive collaboration, it is vital to help them make connections to see how they might use them in a more constructive way. While this type of action game might help students learn communication and collaborative skills, some have more educational applications than others.

A quick Google Search will yield many other online games. However, it is important to have an instructional strategy as some are better used for skill practice, rather than critical thinking and/or problem-solving. For example, in Mr. Nussbaum's Slalom (2015), an online math action game, players achieve an Olympic-style medal based upon their ability to navigate the slalom gates' math problems to get the correct answers and are given a timed score with seconds subtracted for mistakes. By completing math problems in a specific amount of time, they are practicing math facts, but not necessarily thinking critically.

Role-Playing Games

Entertainment role-playing games (RPGs) have moved from nonelectronic dungeons and dragons games to very complex *massively multiplayer online role-playing games* (MMORPG). In RPGs, the story is really the foundation and players take on a role within the story. Commercial RPGs are generally similar to action games in that warfare, conflict, and competition are elements. However, emphasis is placed upon collaboration and cooperation as players often have to work together to achieve the games' goals.

Commercial RPGs, such as World of Warcraft (Blizzard Entertainment, Inc., 2015), have been integrated into classrooms with some success for gains in academic objectives. Young et al. (2012) described how MMPORGs were used for language learning, stating: "Language allows players to negotiate meaning for action within the game context, and the power of video games for language learning is attributed to this grounded use of language in context" (p. 75).

Darfur is Dying (MTVU, 2009) teaches students about the conflict in the Darfur region of Sudan by allowing them to play the role of a Darfurian who must keep his or her refugee camp functioning by foraging for water and escaping capture by the rebels. Peacemaker (Impact Games, 2012), which teaches students about the Israeli-Palestinian conflict, has players choose to play either the Israeli prime minister or the Palestinian president in trying to solve this age-old conflict.

Classcraft (Classcraft Studios, Inc., 2014) is an online RPG designed after Word of Warcraft, to help teachers with their classroom management by improving students' engagement, performance, and leadership and collaboration skills. Students role-play three different characters (i.e., Healer, Mage, or Warrior) and gain or lose points based upon their actual classroom behavior and achievements. Teachers can sign up their class for free, but there are also upgrades for a paid subscription.

Strategy Games

Traditional strategy games, such as chess, are the foundation for today's video strategy games. Like chess, players in these digital games use strategy and/or tactics to outmaneuver their opponents in single-player, multiplayer, or massively multiplayer online versions. Players move their avatars, armies, troops, and equipment from a map or world view, which provides a more strategic perspective.

There are two types of strategy games: turn-based, where players take turns, and real-time continuous play. While some strategy games focus strictly on tactics where the player acts as a tactician to best utilize his or her combat troops in a specific battle, others include action elements as well. For example, America's Army (Department of Defense, 2015) requires a lot of tactical and strategic decisions to move troops around and it also includes a great deal of multiplayer first-person shooter-style action.

Simulation Games

SimCity (Electronic Arts, 2014), which was first developed in the mid-1980s, provides a virtual environment where players build simulated cities and communities. This game has been integrated into science, technology, engineering, and math by classroom teachers. Today students can engage with others within the multiplayer global market. Other simulation games provide opportunities for players to engage with peers in a virtual environment where they create avatars and navigate through a virtual world.

Second Life (Linden Research, 2015) allows nonprofit organizations and medical, training, and educational institutions to create a virtual venue for meetings, courses, and trainings. Many schools have created Second Life virtual campuses where students can meet, create, and interact. Simulations of this nature can provide opportunities for them to practice observational skills and decision-making. While simulations can be very helpful, especially in critical learning environments, such as a surgeon in a medical trauma unit, they can also be used to help students learn to make appropriate academic and life decisions.

GAMIFICATION

Gamification is a term used for adding gaming elements to instruction, which can stimulate student engagement and learning when done properly. Tu et al. (2015) provided a model for gamifying existing curriculum that includes: (a) goal setting, where players set goals for the game; (b) player engagement, where players get a sense of their game personality (i.e., what motivates them—intrinsic or extrinsic); (c) progressive design, where players get a sense of progress through the cycle of motivation, action, and feedback; and (d) environment building, where players work collaboratively in teams or communities.

The classic Decisions-Decisions (Scholastic, 2015) combines simulation, scenario, and role-playing. Students work in teams and play the role of a mayor of a small town with an environmental problem. In the scenario, the town's water was being polluted and its biggest employer is being accused. Acting as the mayor, students have to come to a consensus on identifying and prioritizing three goals: (a) support the town's environment, (b) support the town's economy, or (c) get reelected as mayor. This often required a rigorous discussion between teammates as to *why* they wanted to choose their priorities.

One might consider the Decisions-Decisions series as an example of the gamification of curriculum. First, students set their goals for the game by setting their priorities. While there isn't an explicit player engagement element within this game design, students have to discuss the reasons *why* they set their priorities as they did, thus identifying their gaming personality. There is also progressive design because it provides an engagement loop of motivation, action, and feedback. Environment building was also an element as students worked collaboratively, negotiating individual ideas among themselves to make the best possible decision.

Adding some gamification elements of goal setting, player engagement, progressive design, and environment building to existing curricula is also an option. Think about gamifying a unit by adding these elements: (a) students setting their curricular goals, (b) students getting a sense of what motivates them (i.e., intrinsic or extrinsic), (c) students gaining a sense of their progress, and (d) students building an environment and developing a sense of community by working together.

GAMIFYING RESOURCES

- The Gamification Guide for Teachers. http://elearningindustry.com/the-gamification-guide-for-teachers
- Gamifying My Classroom. http://gamifyingmyclass.com
- Get Your Game On: How to Build Curriculum Units Using the Video Game Model. http://www.edutopia.org/blog/gamification-game-based-learning-unit-andrew-miller
- Gamification at the Curriculum Level. http://www.trainingindustry.com/blog/blog-entries/gamification-at-the-curriculum-level.aspx
- Gamification: Games and Curriculum. TEQ: It's All about Learning. http://www.teq.com/blog/2015/06/gamification-games-curriculum-part-5-6/#.VbFfpflD5ko

SCENARIO: LEARNING WITH GAMES—
VIRTUAL MANIPULATIVES

Sally teaches at an elementary school where she rotates with her students, beginning in kindergarten and then staying with them through second grade. She has been making her students use Cuisenaire rods as math manipulatives to learn base-ten *place value*, which is a foundational math principle that is embedded from kindergarten onward.

Specifically, kindergarten students should be able to "Work with numbers 11–19 to gain foundations for place value" (p. 10). For grade 1, students should be able to "Extend the counting sequence, Understand place value, and Use place value understanding and properties" (p. 14). For grade 2, students should be able to "Understand place value, Use place value understanding and properties of operations to add and subtract" (Common Core, 2015, p. 18).

In doing some searching for lessons that integrate technology to teach base-ten place value, she came across several math resources to help students meet these Common Core Math Standards. She thought that these might work well and had heard of students using more complex virtual manipulatives that promote and expand their understanding of math. She was beginning a rotation with new kindergartners and thought that this would be the perfect time to enhance her math curriculum with some fun games.

Sally thought that by starting in kindergarten, her students could begin with traditional Cuisenaire rods as math manipulatives to learn base-ten *place value* and then move into the virtual manipulatives using either online or iPad app-based ten games. For example, ABCya.com (2016) provides a game that would work well. Figure 10.1 illustrates how students can use the virtual manipulatives on the computer or iPad.

Once the students understand the foundations of base ten, Sally can increase the level of difficulty. For example, having students play Base Ten Bingo requires them to count the virtual manipulatives and then match them with the numerical value as shown in figure 10.2.

She also found that the Illuminations website by National Council of Teachers of Mathematics (NCTM) (2016) has many lessons that are directly aligned to NCTM and the Common Core Math Standards, for all grade levels. In addition, they offer many interactive virtual manipulatives, as shown in figure 10.3, for computers and mobile devices, which her students could use on the set of class of iPads she has just received.

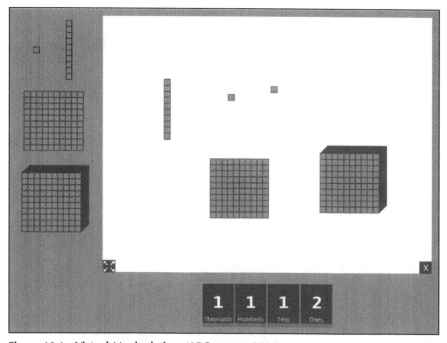

Figure 10.1   Virtual Manipulatives (ABCya.com, 2016)

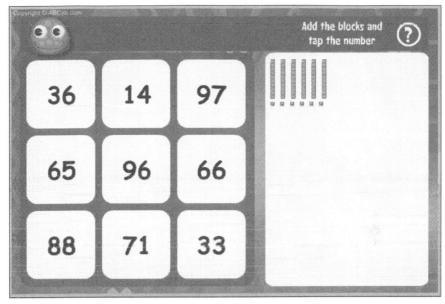

Figure 10.2   Base Ten BINGO (ABCya.com, 2016)

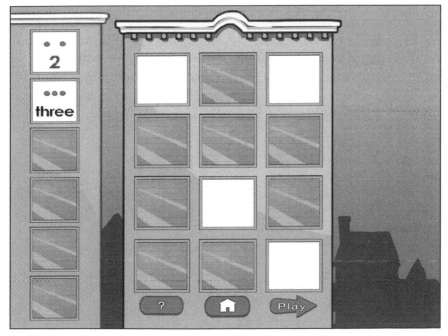

Figure 10.3   Math Concentration (NCTM, Illuminations, 2016)

SUMMARY

The purpose of this chapter was to provide an overview or foundation of research, the types of video games, and the issues or concerns when games are integrated into the classroom. It's important to remember that research on video game play for learning suggests that it is a very complex topic. Some even suggest that video games can become an addiction and/or that playing violent video games can enhance violent behavior.

On the contrary, there are others who suggest that video game play in the classroom motivates student engagement and provides opportunities for technology-enhanced learning. This chapter also provided examples of how games might be used for instruction, in safe ways, including gamification and the elements that help educators gamify curriculum.

The scenario in this chapter provided an example of how online and iPad games could be integrated into math curriculum to help students achieve Common Core Math Standards. It is important to remember, however, that within this scenario, the teacher has the opportunity to loop with her kindergarten students through second grade. This would allow her to build upon having the students use various games to enhance their understanding of math over three years. While most teachers won't have that opportunity, these types of games can be used in early elementary schooling to help students gain a more concrete understanding of base-ten place value.

While the chapter provided ways to integrate gaming into the classroom, as with all instructional strategies that integrate digital tools, it's important to have a foundation that supports students learning. In other words, integrating digital games might well be cool or fun, but the main purpose is to help students learn.

REFERENCES AND RESOURCES

ABCya.Com, LLC. (2016). Educational games and apps for kids. Retrieved from: http://www.abcya.com/.

Anderson, C. A., Shibuya, A., Ihori, N., Swing, E. L., Bushman, B. J., Sakamoto, A., Rothstein, H. R., and Saleem, M. (2010). Violent video game effects on aggression, empathy, and prosocial behavior in eastern and western countries: A meta-analytic review. *Psychological Bulletin, 136* (2), 151.

Bavelier, D., Green, S., Han, D., Renshaw, P., Merzenich, M., and Gentile, D. (2011). Brains on video games. *Nature Reviews Neuroscience, 12* (12), 763–68.

Bethesda Softworks LLC. (2015). Skyrim. Retrieved from: http://www.elderscrolls.com/skyrim/.

Blades, R., (2013). Gaming and History: Civilization V and the Law of Accelerating Returns. Humanities, Arts, Science, Technology Alliance and Collaboratory. Retrieved from: http://www.hastac.org/blogs/rblades/2013/01/06/gaming-and-history-civilization-v-and-law-accelerating-returns.

Blizzard Entertainment, Inc. (2013). Beginner's Guide—Game Guide—World of Warcraft. Retrieved from: http://us.battle.net/wow/en/game/guide/.

Classcraft Studios, Inc. (2014). Make Learning an Adventure. Retrieved from: http://www.classcraft.com.

Common Core: State Standards Initiative. (2015). Mathematics Standards. Retrieved from: http://www.corestandards.org/Math/.

Dai, D. Y., and Wind, A. P., (2011). Computer games and opportunity to learn: Implications from low socioeconomic backgrounds. In S. Tobias and J. D. Fletcher (eds.), *Computer games and instruction* (pp. 477–500).

Department of Defense. (2015). America's Army. Retrieved from: http://www.americasarmy.com/.

Electronic Arts, Inc. (2014). SimCity. Retrieved from: http://www.simcity.com.

Grüsser, S. M., Thalemann, R., and Griffiths, M. D. (2006). Excessive computer game playing: Evidence for addiction and aggression? *CyberPsychology & Behavior, 10* (2), 290–92.

Houghton Mifflin Harcourt. (2015). Oregon Trail. Retrieved from: http://www.hmhco.com/at-home/featured-shops/the-learning-company/oregon-trail.

Impact Games. (2012). PeaceMaker: Play the News, Solve the Puzzle. Retrieved from: http://www.impactgames.com/peacemaker.php.

Kirschner, P. A., Sweller, J., and Clark, R. E. (2006). Why minimal guidance during instruction does not work: An analysis of the failure of constructivist, discovery, problem-based, experiential, and inquiry-based teaching. *Educational Psychologist, 41*, 75–76.

Klahr, D., and Nigam, M. (2004). The equivalence of learning paths in early science instruction. *Psychological Science, 15* (10), 661–67.

Linden Research, Inc. (2015). Second Life. Retrieved from: http://secondlife.com.

Mayer, R. E. (2004). Should there be a three-strikes rule against pure discovery learning? The case for guided methods of instruction. *American Psychologist, 59*, 14–19.

MrNussbaum.Com. (2015). Mr.N's Math Slalom—A 3 D Math Skiing Game for Kids. Retrieved from: http://mrnussbaum.com/slalom/.

MTVU. (2013). Darfur Is Dying—Play mtvU's Darfur refugee game for change. Retrieved from: http://www.darfurisdying.com/aboutgame.html.

National Council for the Social Studies (NCSS), the College, Career, and Civic Life (C3) Framework for Social Studies State Standards: Guidance for Enhancing the Rigor of K–12 Civics, Economics, Geography, and History (Silver Spring, MD: NCSS, 2013).

National Council of Teachers of Mathematics. (NCTM). (2016). Illuminations: Resources for teaching math. Retrieved from: http://illuminations.nctm.org/.

Resnick, M. (2004). Edutainment? No thanks. I prefer playful learning. *Associazione Civita Report on Edutainment, 14*.

Scholastic. (2015). Decisions-Decisions: Environment by Tom Snyder Productions. Retrieved from: http://teacher.scholastic.com/products/tomsnyder.htm.

Schwartz, K. (2014). Bypassing the Textbook: Video Games Transform Social Studies Curriculum. In Mind/Shift. KQED News. Retrieved from: http://ww2.kqed.org/mindshift/2014/01/16/forget-the-textbook-video-games-as-social-studies-content/.

Take-Two Interactive Software. (2010). Retrieved from: http://www.civilization5. com/.

Tu, C. H., Sujo-Montes, L. E., and Yen, C. J. (2015). Gamification for Learning. In *Media Rich Instruction* (pp. 203–217). New York: Springer International Publishing.

Van Eck, R. (2009). A guide to integrating COTS games into your classroom. *Handbook of Research on Effective Electronic Gaming in Education*, 1.

Young, M. F., Slota, S. T., Cutter, A. B., Jalette, G, Mullin, G., Lai, B., Simeoni, Z., Tran, T., and Yukhymenko, M. (2012). Our princess is in another castle: A review of trends in serious gaming for education. *Review of Educational Research, 82* (1), 61–89.

Yousafzai, S., Hussain, Z., and Griffiths, M. (2013). Social responsibility in online videogaming: What should the videogame industry do? *Addiction Research & Theory*, 1–5.

Index

Page references for figures are italicized.

About the Author

As an educator for more than thirty-five years, **Michael Blocher**, PhD, has taught in a variety of classrooms. His teaching experiences span from third grade elementary classroom teacher to doctoral dissertation chair. His research interests include learner engagement in online learning environments, technology integration into the curriculum, technology-based instructional media, and gaming for learning. He has published articles and book chapters and presented numerous papers on topics within the field of educational technology, both nationally and internationally.

Blocher currently serves as professor of educational technology in Northern Arizona University's College of Education faculty where he teaches face-to-face and online undergraduate-, masters-, and doctoral-level courses. He especially enjoys teaching the Computers in the Classroom course for undergraduate students in Northern Arizona University's teacher preparation program. Over the years, he has noticed that his students have changed and now come into his class with considerable technology skills. However, teachers often struggle with planning lessons where technology is used by the students in ways that support their achievement of academic standards. This book was written in response to his desire to provide foundational information and examples of how teachers can design lessons and units wherein their students can use today's digital tools to help them enhance their knowledge.

Summaries + Case Studies from Book -

group vs individual learning
relationship of teacher to students

K ————————→ 8   (artifical, not necessary
                    development categorized)

hard   soft
scaffolding   scaffolding

"instruction"   "facilitating"

individual   group
building blocks   application
Teacher "toys" -

Tech is changing us as humans, how we relate (or not)
to each other, how we learn (or not) / process info; attention
                                                        spans

What we know about learning...
Ultimately, learning is both social + individual
Use of all senses
3D better than 2D
Cumulative
Requires both info + process.
Affective components

Goal of teach-speed / efficiency
Motivation of Tech Companies - $ $
How much?
Are computer skills necessary in K-8?

Digital Assessments / Standardized or online
           quizzes / exams (assessing
                            computer
                   knowledge or subject mastery?)